Heart of a Forerunner

How to Be a Relevant and Influential Voice in a Wayward Nation

FOA

Cover design by Benjamin Rogers

ISBN-9798844215704
Imprint: Independently Published

Contents

Contents

FORWARD

Dave Warn
Founder, *Forerunners of America*
Host, *INSIGHTS Podcast*

FORWARD BY DAVE WARN

CHARACTERISTICS & QUALITIES OF A FORERUNNER

A travesty of contemporary Christianity is that the role of a forerunner has been all but forgotten! Simply put, a forerunner is somebody who goes before someone or something else. However, within the context of Scripture, a forerunner is a cultural influencer who serves an essential role in God's redemptive purposes. Having given my life to pursue a forerunner lifestyle, allow me to first highlight some important characteristics of a forerunner's calling and then close with some forerunner heart qualities.

In the book of Luke, an angel announces to John the Baptist's father that John will grow up to be a forerunner:

And he will turn many of the sons of Israel back to the Lord their God. It is he who will go <u>as a forerunner</u> before Him [Jesus] in the spirit and power of Elijah, to turn the hearts of the fathers back to the children, and the disobedient to the attitude of the righteous, so as to make

> *ready a people prepared for the Lord* (Luke 1:16–17, NASB, emphasis added).

John's forerunner calling was centered on influencing culture by seeing lives and families changed to be prepared to meet their Messiah.

How did John seek to accomplish this calling? A brief overview of John's ministry reveals three important characteristics. First, John understood the times in which he lived. He was familiar with the wayward hearts of the people, the evil in government, and the hypocrisy of religious leaders (Luke 3:7–8, 18–20; Matt. 3:7). Also, he understood that God had called him to confront each of these aspects of culture. Moreover, he knew that he was to proclaim that the Messiah was about to take center stage. To be effective forerunners today, we too must discern what is taking place in our culture, address it, and understand what the Bible says about the days in which we are living.

Second, John warned the people of the serious nature of their situation. John declared, *"Even now the ax of God's judgment is poised, ready to sever the roots of the trees. Yes, every tree that does not produce good fruit will be chopped down and thrown into the fire,"* and, *"Someone is coming soon who is greater than I am ... He is ready to separate the chaff from the wheat with his winnowing fork. Then he will clean up the threshing area, gathering the wheat into his barn but burning the chaff with never-ending fire"* (Matt. 3:10–12). Warning others about the consequences of meeting a holy God with an unrepentant heart is also foundational to being a forerunner. Today, most Christian leaders won't address waywardness and the judgment it elicits. In our current Christian environment, such preaching is often viewed as extreme, unloving, and unnecessary. Nonetheless, after three and half decades of speaking in many locations, I've noticed that just the opposite is true. It is these very messages that free the most people and bear lasting fruit.

Furthermore, John helped people respond in faith. It is one thing to understand cultural issues and to warn people about difficulty ahead; it is quite another to show people the way forward. Yet John did this too by specifically explaining what it would look like to turn to God in repentance and be saved from the coming judgment (Luke 3:10–14). As an act of faith, he told the general population to forsake self-centeredness and greed by sharing their food and clothes with others. When Roman soldiers came under conviction of sin, John told them, *"Don't extort money or make false accusations. And be content with your pay."* Similarly, he told the tax collectors to forsake corruption by telling them to *"collect no more taxes than the government requires."* Providing people with hope by helping them embrace God's will and ways is also a foundational characteristic of an effective forerunner.

In summary, understanding the culture and warning the people while challenging people to turn from sin and turn to God are vital characteristics of a forerunner. Throughout this book, you are about to see these themes greatly expanded!

Beyond John's example, Scripture presents other exemplary forerunners. As a preacher of righteousness,

Noah became the Bible's first forerunner when he saw what was coming, built an ark, and *"warned the world of God's righteous judgment"* (2 Pet. 2:5). Moses, having received a "now" message from God for the Hebrews (Deut. 31:16–19), understood the hearts of the people, saw what was coming, and composed a song of warning as his final testament to the nation of Israel (Deut. 32). Likewise, Jeremiah proclaimed God's message of warning and His call to repentance before the arrival of devastating national judgment (Jer. 3:11–14; 11:1–17). The apostle Peter warned the people and preached repentance, *"strongly urging all his listeners, 'Save yourselves from this crooked generation!'"* (Acts 2:40). Even Jesus was a forerunner who served as the ultimate example of one who prepared people to stand before a holy God (Heb. 6:19–20). Each of these people confronted the culture and influenced multitudes through their lives and message.

Not every one of us are called to influence multitudes, but our calling is no less important. The vast majority of us are called to be forerunners to our families, friends, churches, neighbors, and co-workers. In other words, once we are awakened to God's "now" message, we will be expected to influence those around us.

Where, then, does this forerunner journey begin? As highlighted in the book title, it begins in the heart. God will not share His "now" message with just anyone. Instead, the psalmist teaches, *"The secrets of the Lord are for those who fear Him"* (Psa. 25:14, NASB). Therefore, it is vital that you read the following pages with a willingness to receive what

God has to say to our nation and with a reverent heart that trembles at God's Word (Isa. 66:2).

Crucial as the fear of the Lord is to develop a forerunner heart, it is not the only necessary quality. Observing forerunners throughout the Bible, we find other outstanding qualities such as humility, truthfulness, perseverance, and living full of faith. If we hope to receive all that God has in store for us to make a difference in our generation, then the same qualities must be true of us.

Once again, highlighting John the Baptist's example, John feared the Lord, not even wanting to untie Jesus' sandals because he saw himself as unworthy (Mark 1:7). In humility, John willingly and joyfully stepped down from his ministry position, having accomplished his role in preparing the way for Jesus to takeover. Rather than become possessive of his disciples, he pointed them to follow Jesus (John 1:35–37). Also, John's selfless statement cannot be emphasized enough: *"He [Jesus] must become greater and greater, and I must become less and less"* (John 3:30).

Furthermore, John was not impressed with himself or with others, and this empowered him to repeatedly speak the truth, regardless of the response. Not only did he call the religious leaders and the crowds "a brood of vipers" (Matt. 3:7; Luke 3:7), but he also fearlessly rebuked King Herod for marrying his brother's wife (Mark 6:17-18). John confronted people with the truth, knowing that kings, religious leaders, and the crowds needed to be awakened to the severity of their sin problem and repent. Many did. Others did not. Either way, John presented the truth and left the results to

God. Oh, that God may raise up forerunners with similar courage in our day!

Not only did John have a heart that feared the Lord, embraced humility, and fearlessly spoke the truth; he also persevered. After an enormously fruitful ministry baptizing the masses at the Jordan River and seeing the Holy Spirit descend upon Jesus as a dove, John found himself in prison. While in confinement, he came to a crisis of faith, wrestling over whether Jesus was truly the Messiah, and he sent his disciples to question Jesus. Upon their return, John appears to have accepted Jesus' response. In fact, he would later die for asserting God's righteous decrees. Clearly, the heart of a forerunner includes persevering through doubts and difficulties—even through persecution.

Last, John lived a life full of faith. Not intimidated by anyone, John told everyone to repent—whether they were the king, prominent leaders, Roman soldiers, or commoners. Then, as it is now, repentance was not a popular message. Repentance implies that something is wrong—not only wrong within the culture but wrong within each individual heart—yet John walked with God in great faith, declaring this message to his generation.

Like John, sometimes I find myself full of faith and experiencing wonderful ministry results, and occasionally I also find myself doubting God and struggling through various challenges. However, in my moments of weakness, the fear of the Lord, humility, a focus on the truth, and perseverance are keys to bring my heart back to a place where I can receive God's "now" message for our generation and can once again become full of faith to influence those around me.

As you read the following pages, keep these qualities in mind, but most of all, ask God how He may want to develop the heart of a forerunner within you. God has used forerunners throughout history, and it may be that He is calling you to serve as a forerunner in our day!

INTRODUCTION

INTRODUCTION

A FORERUNNER CALLING

For many of us, our fervent heart-cry is to live relevant and influential lives that produce both immediate and eternal fruit. Those of us who feel this way may be sensing God's call upon our lives to serve as His forerunners. What then is this call? Why does it matter? How is it related to our gospel mission? And what practical steps can we take to become cultural influencers? In short, how can we foster the heart of a forerunner?

Simply put, a forerunner is a cultural influencer who serves an essential role in God's redemptive purposes. Perhaps America's most renown forerunner is Abraham Lincoln. Nearly two and a half centuries after the pilgrims established a community of believers to be *"a city on a hill"* that would reflect God's glory to the nations of the world (Matt. 5:14), President Lincoln understood how far America had departed from the vision of our forebearers. Moreover, he recognized the Civil War as God's divine judgment upon our nation:

> Fondly do we hope—fervently do we pray—that this mighty scourge of war may speedily pass away. Yet, if God wills that it continue, until all the wealth piled by the bond-man's two hundred and fifty years of unrequited toil shall be sunk, and until every drop of blood drawn with the lash, shall be paid by another drawn with the sword, as was said three thousand years ago, so still it must be said "the judgments of the Lord, are true and righteous altogether."[1]

Two years into the war, President Lincoln served as a forerunner to our divided nation when he proclaimed April 30, 1863 as a national day of fasting and prayer. Lincoln's bold words are similar in tone to the Old Testament prophets who called the people to repentance:

> We have been the recipients of the choicest bounties of Heaven. We have been preserved, these many years, in peace and prosperity. We have grown in numbers, wealth and power, as no other nation has ever grown. But we have forgotten God. We have forgotten the gracious hand which preserved us in peace, and multiplied and enriched and strengthened us; and we have vainly imagined, in the deceitfulness of our hearts, that all these blessings were produced by some superior wisdom and virtue of our own. Intoxicated with unbroken success, we have become too self-sufficient to feel the necessity of redeeming and preserving grace, too proud to pray to the God that made us!

> It behooves us then, to humble ourselves before the offended Power, to confess our national sins, and to pray for clemency and forgiveness.[2]

The Civil War accrued more American deaths than any other war before or since. If ever there was a time for a forerunner to present a national message, this was it. Fortunately, Lincoln rose to the occasion and encouraged the nation to honestly evaluate itself and to seek God for mercy. He understood the day and hour in which he was living, warned the people, and helped them respond in faith by setting aside a specific day to repent, fast, and pray.

Likewise, do we, today, recognize how far our nation has veered away from its original goal of serving as a city on a hill that reflects God's glory to the nations of the world, drawing the hearts of people back to God? Do we understand the national consequences of our waywardness? Are we capable of recognizing God's judgment? Do we have a message of hope for others? In short, can we discern the day and hour in which we are living? And do we know enough to guide others into God's redemptive purpose for America in times of blessing *and* in times of difficulty?

As we seek to respond to God's call, let us endeavor to develop the heart of a forerunner by first ensuring that we understand God's redemptive purpose for nations. Then, let us evaluate America's perilous trajectory. Only after considering this foundation will we be equipped to have an informed response to God's call to us to become relevant and influential voices in our nation. Finally, let us examine practical steps for becoming cultural influencers who are prepared for what lies ahead.

Part 1

THE REDEMPTIVE ROLE OF NATIONS

CHAPTER 1

A DOMINION MANDATE

Having uniquely designed humanity to serve as His stewards over creation, God bestowed upon Adam and Eve both a blessing and a charge:

> *Then God said, "Let us make man in our image, after our likeness. And let them have dominion over the fish of the sea and over the birds of the heavens and over the livestock and over all the earth and over every creeping thing that creeps on the earth." So God created man in his own image, in the image of God he created him; male and female he created them. And God blessed them. And God said to them, "Be fruitful and multiply and fill the earth and subdue it, and have dominion over the fish of the sea and over the birds of the heavens and over every living thing that moves on the earth"* (Gen. 1:27–28, ESV).

Variously titled by theologians, this dominion mandate is both humanity's purpose statement and receipt of divine authority. In short, it is our original commission.

How exactly this dominion was to be executed in an orderly manner as humanity multiplied is not explicitly stated. Instead, the text focuses on the institution of family units through the establishment of marriage and independent households:

> *Then the LORD God said, "It is not good for the man to be alone. I will make a helper who is just right for him." ... So the LORD God caused the man to fall into a deep sleep. While the man slept, the LORD God took out one of the man's ribs and closed up the opening. Then the LORD God made a woman from the rib, and he brought her to the man.*
>
> *"At last!" the man exclaimed.*
>
> *"This one is bone from my bone,*
> *and flesh from my flesh!"*
> *She will be called 'woman,'*
> *because she was taken from 'man.'"*
>
> *This explains why a man leaves his father and mother and is joined to his wife, and the two are united into one"* (Gen. 2:18, 21–24).

Notably, God's dominion mandate failed to grant us authority over other humans outside of our family households. Presumably, communities would eventually form around common interests in our effort to govern creation. In his book *God and the Nations*, Henry Morris argues that humanity's mandate to steward creation necessitates the development of the disciplines we today call culture:

- Science (to understand how to control creation)

- Technology (to control creation)
- Commerce (for effective implementation of science and technology)
- Education (to effectively transmit knowledge and skills)
- Fine arts (to glorify our Creator and King)[3]

The development of such culture would necessitate sizeable communities of people, but these communities would function according to a mutual respect for one another and for the greater purpose of stewarding God's creation. They would not be held in check by fear of a governing authority's ability to punish them. Morris concludes:

> At that time there theoretically would be no need for such occupations as the military, law enforcement, or other such governmental agencies.
>
> In fact, as far as the record goes, in the Edenic world as intended by the Creator, there would have been no government necessary at all, except the patriarchal system, with the father as head of each family and with his wife as a *"help"* [mate] for him. Presumably as each son grew to manhood and took a wife, he would then *"cleave to"* her, leaving his father and mother and thus establishing his own family unit. Society would eventually consist of many families, each with its own head, working together to honor God and serve mankind.
>
> But such an idyllic society never actually existed, because Satan and the entrance of sin into the world

complicated the world before the process of filling it could begin.[4]

With the introduction of sin, humanity's unified purpose was supplanted by competing self-interests (Gen. 3). Humanity devolved into a state of perpetual wickedness and violence, ultimately compelling God to intervene with a sweeping judgment that virtually reset humanity (Gen. 6). Our dominion mandate would be preserved, but God's original intent would be notably amended (Gen. 9:1–7). This time, God's dominion mandate would authorize human government.

CHAPTER 2

HUMAN GOVERNMENT ESTABLISHED

Noah's flood is the Bible's first example of severe judgment, which is the final judgment upon a rebellious people who simply refuse to respond to God's corrective judgments (Gen. 6:11–13, 17). The imagery of the flood account echoes the creation account, conveying a sense that God's heart in this judgment was to restore the goodness of His creation. In a *Bible Project* blog, Andy Patton explains:

> Genesis describes the flood as the de-creation of the world—the earth sinks back into the chaotic waters that God cleared away on page one of the Bible (Genesis 1:6–10). In the ark, God carries Noah's family through the flood unharmed to start afresh in a world returned to innocence. It is a new beginning and a chance to have a different end. ... God was acting to restore the goodness of his creation. God preserves one family through the flood and elevates Noah as a new Adam, placed once

again in a garden on a high mountain paradise with the commission to be fruitful and multiply.[5]

As Noah and his family entered this restored creation, God renewed his charge to humanity by reiterating the dominion mandate—except this time it was slightly different. This time it was tailored for stewarding a world governed by death:

> *And God blessed Noah and his sons and said to them, "Be fruitful and multiply and fill the earth. The fear of you and the dread of you shall be upon every beast of the earth and upon every bird of the heavens, upon everything that creeps on the ground and all the fish of the sea. Into your hand they are delivered.* ***Every moving thing that lives shall be food for you.*** *And as I gave you the green plants, I give you everything. But you shall not eat flesh with its life, that is, its blood.*
>
> ***And for your lifeblood I will require a reckoning****: from every beast I will require it and from man. From his fellow man I will require a reckoning for the life of man. 'Whoever sheds the blood of man, by man shall his blood be shed, for God made man in his own image'"* (Gen. 9:1–6, ESV, emphasis added).

For the first time, God granted humanity limited authority to take life—even human life. By conferring such authority, God also implicitly charged humanity with the responsibility to preserve human life. In order to protect life in a creation corrupted by sin, humanity would need to focus not only on the cultural disciplines needed to control animals and the environment, but also on the administrative disciplines necessary to control the types of human behavior that could lead to murder. These include behaviors like robbery, extortion, adultery, rape, slander, assault and battery, etc. Henry Morris concludes:

> Some kind of government would be necessary, and this would imply that many new types of vocations were now called for. Not only government bureaucrats, but also policemen, judges, lawyers, legislators, and others necessary for a functioning government are implied. Some kind of military establishment is also warranted. Thus, the dominion mandate not only authorizes but anticipates every form of human activity that is honorable and useful in the service of God and man.[6]

CHAPTER 3

ORIGIN OF NATIONS

A global system of nations united in purpose could have been an effective means of fulfilling humanity's dominion mandate. Instead, we find that humanity's collective efforts were soon channeled into another act of rebellion: *"Then they said, 'Come, let's build a great city for ourselves with a tower that reaches into the sky. This will make us famous and keep us from being scattered all over the world'"* (Gen. 11:4).

Shortly after experiencing a global flood that was released to cleanse the earth of its wickedness, humanity again forfeited its renewed opportunity to steward God's creation in submission to His will. Contravening their charge in Genesis 9:1 to spread out and fill the earth, the people determined to congregate in a magnificent city where, far from being thankful for their second chance at obedience, they chose to honor themselves rather than God.

Romans 1 provides further insight into their mindset and motivations, *"Yes, they knew God, but they wouldn't worship him as God or even give him thanks. And they began to think up foolish ideas of what God was like. As a result, their minds became dark and confused"* (Rom. 1:21). Because of this, God abandoned humanity to its futile ideas, ultimately permitting us to become enslaved to our passions and desires: *"Since they thought it foolish to acknowledge God, he abandoned them to their foolish thinking and let them do things that should never be done. Their lives became full of every kind of wickedness"* (Rom. 1:28–29b).

Moreover, God foiled humanity's rebellious plan by dividing its language (Gen. 11:5–9). The ensuing confusion compelled people to spread throughout the world. More importantly, it limited their ability to collectively rebel against God. It was in this judgment at Babel that God established nations defined by language and geographic borders. This is affirmed in Deuteronomy 32:8, *"When the Most High assigned lands to the nations, when he divided up the human race, he established the boundaries of the peoples according to the number in his heavenly court."*

Thus, nations were birthed in rebellion, and they exist as a perpetual reminder that humanity's dominion over creation is derived from the Creator God who reigns as King. As such, all nations belong to God and are subject to His will (Psa. 82:8).

CHAPTER 4

PURPOSE OF NATIONS

God may have established nations in judgment, but His heart was filled with mercy. God's intent was not only to limit humanity's ability to collectively rebel against Him but also to draw the hearts of the people back to Himself. In short, God has a redemptive role for nations.

Nations were formed when God divided humanity by confusing the language:

> *"Look!" [God] said. "The people are united, and they all speak the same language. After this, nothing they set out to do will be impossible for them! Come, let's go down and confuse the people with different languages. Then they won't be able to understand each other."*
>
> *In that way, the LORD scattered them all over the world, and they stopped building the city. That is why the city was called Babel, because that is where the LORD confused the people with different languages. In this way he scattered them all over the world"* (Gen. 11:6–9).

By confusing the language, God compelled the people to spread out and fill the earth as He had originally instructed (Gen. 1:28; 9:1). Elsewhere, we learn that God governed this dispersion by guiding each people group into a territory specially selected for them: *"When the Most High assigned lands to the nations, when he divided up the human race, he established the boundaries of the people"* (Deut. 32:8a).

Despite having abandoned humanity to its lusts and passions (Rom. 1:24), God remained intimately involved in the stories of these nations: *"From one man [God] created all the nations throughout the whole earth. He decided beforehand when they should rise and fall, and he determined their boundaries. 'His purpose was for the nations to seek after God and perhaps feel their way toward him and find him—though he is not far from any one of us'"* (Acts 17:26–27). Throughout history, God has governed the rise and fall of nations. At times we might be tempted to question why God permitted various difficulties, but we are told that God's purpose behind every national event is ultimately an effort to draw the hearts of people back to Himself.

In the very next chapter of the Bible, after recounting the origin of nations, God expresses His heart to Abram: *"All the families on earth will be blessed through you"* (Gen. 12:3). God supernaturally built Abram into the nation of Israel to further His plan of redemption by becoming the recipients of God's special revelation and His Messiah. Certainly, the remnant of Israel has served a unique role, but Acts 17:26–27 reveals that every nation has played—and continues to play—an important part in God's redemptive plan. God is actively involved in the affairs of every nation as He endeavors to draw the hearts of mankind to Himself.

CHAPTER 5

WHEN GOD TROUBLES A NATION

The apostle Paul teaches that God's purpose for creating nations was to draw the hearts of people back to Himself (Acts 17:26–27). An example of this can be found in the story of King Asa. God explains to Asa that, in the days of Israel's judges, He had troubled the nation with every kind of distress and with international military pressure:

> *"For a long time Israel was without the true God, without a priest to teach them, and without the Law to instruct them. But whenever they were in trouble and turned to the* Lord, *the God of Israel, and sought him out, they found him.*
>
> *During those dark times, it was not safe to travel. Problems troubled the people of every land. Nation fought against nation, and city against city, for God was troubling them with every kind of problem"* (2 Chron. 15:3–6).

The people and their leaders were placed in such distressing situations that they were compelled to either draw near to God in obedience or utterly forsake the Lord. Indeed, the book of Judges is replete with Israel's cyclical pattern of rebellion that resulted in God's affliction, thus prompting repentance, which then produced deliverance. God troubled the nation as a means of provoking a change of heart and behavior.

The prophet Azariah revealed to Asa that God was not a helpless bystander in Israel's history. Moreover, He did not blame the nation's troubles upon its political policies. Certainly, we can assume that God used poor political decisions to accomplish His purposes, but God declares that it was ultimately He who permitted every kind of problem to arise within the nation, and that it was both a judgment and an act of mercy. In other words, God was not content to abandon the nation when it rejected Him. Instead, God did what was necessary to alert the people to their rebellion in order that He might redeem them and restore them to their true purpose.

Azariah exhorts King Asa, *"The LORD will stay with you as long as you stay with him! Whenever you seek him, you will find him. But if you abandon him, he will abandon you"* (2 Chron. 15:2). Just as in the days of Israel's judges, deliverance could be found in the time of King Asa if the people would seek God. In his commentary on Chronicles, Old Testament scholar John Thompson writes:

> It was not that Asa needed courage to face another war but to undertake more fully a reform he had begun

> earlier. His reform program began at the start of his reign, but he was young and not able to resist the influence of his mother, Maacah, who encouraged various illegitimate religious practices (cf. v. 16). ... [I]t is clear that it was the prophecy of Azariah (v. 1) that gave Asa the courage he needed in the face of his powerful mother to remove the abominable idols from the whole land of Judah and Benjamin and from the towns he had captured in the hills of Ephraim.[7]

Unfortunately, sometimes God must trouble a nation before it is willing to look beyond itself. National crises, boundary disputes, and poor leadership are tools that God uses to alert us to the destructive consequences of our disobedience while there still remains time for repentance. Even when it appears God has turned against a nation or has abandoned it to experience the consequences of its decisions, God remains nearby, calling the people to set aside their rebellion and return to Him.

CHAPTER 6

FUTURE OF NATIONS

God is redeeming His creation. This includes not only individuals but also nations! Far from becoming obsolete at the return of Christ, nations will continue to play an important role in God's redemption story throughout eternity.

God will judge not only individuals upon His return but also nations:

> *"I will gather the armies of the world into the valley of Jehoshaphat. There I will judge them ... Come quickly, all you nations everywhere. Gather together in the valley. ... Let the nations be called to arms. Let them march to the valley of Jehoshaphat. There I, the LORD, will sit to pronounce judgment on them all. ... Thousands upon thousands are waiting in the valley of decision. There the day of the LORD will soon arrive"* (Joel 3:2, 11a, 12, 14).

Likewise, Isaiah prophesies, *"I will gather all nations and peoples together, and they will see my glory"* (Isa. 66:18). At that time, *"The wicked will go down to the grave. This is the fate of all the nations who ignore God"* (Psa. 9:17).

Those nations that remain will serve the Lord: *"People from many nations will come and say, 'Come, let us go up to the mountain of the LORD, to the house of Jacob's God. There he will teach us his ways, and we will walk in his paths.' ... The LORD will mediate between nations and will settle international disputes"* (Isa. 2:3a, 4a).

All of creation is eagerly awaiting this day when God's stewards, restored in our relationship to Him, will finally govern creation in faithful obedience: *"For all creation is waiting eagerly for that future day when God will reveal who his children really are. Against its will, all creation was subjected to God's curse. But with eager hope, the creation looks forward to the day when it will join God's children in glorious freedom from death and decay"* (Rom. 8:19–22).

What began as a response to the destructive influence of sin and as a judgment to hold evil at bay will be redeemed. Human government, and the nations of the world, will provide an organized structure as we fulfill our dominion mandate in a manner that Adam and Eve—or even Noah and his family—could never have fathomed. Ultimately, the nations will become God's eternal means of propagating righteousness throughout His restored creation.

CHAPTER 7

NATIONS IN ETERNITY

"The LORD will be king over all the earth" (Zech. 14:9), but He will not be the only king. Rather, He will reign as King of kings and Lord of lords (Rev. 17:14; 19:16). Isaiah prophesies, *"Look, a righteous king is coming! And honest princes will rule under him"* (Isa. 32:1). Indeed, nations will retain a form of human government with God's faithful servants appointed as kings over nations (Luke 19:12–19). Speaking of the New Jerusalem, Revelation says, *"The nations will walk in its light, and the kings of the world will enter the city in all their glory. ... And all the nations will bring their glory and honor into the city"* (Rev. 21:24, 26).

Implicit in Revelation 21:26 is that nations will preserve their diversity. The glory and splendor of a nation rests in the distinction of its accomplishments, products, and culture. Today, the glory of Greece is its philosophy; the glory of China rests in its architectural wonders, and the glory of America is rooted in its liberties. It would seem that, in God's eternal kingdom, each nation will continue to chart its own course for executing humanity's dominion mandate. This will produce distinction in culture, products, and accomplishments, yet there will be no jealousy because all will be united in purpose.

Having submitted themselves to God, the nations will no longer be motivated by conflicting self-interests. As such, nations will experience lasting peace: *"They will hammer their swords into plowshares and their spears into pruning hooks. Nation will no longer fight against nation, nor train for war anymore"* (Isa. 2:4b).

No longer will there be hostility between nations, nor will there be a need to divide the people's collective efforts as a restraint against evil. Instead, we will live in true obedience to God (Rev. 21:3–4; 22:1–5). Therefore, God will once more unite our language so that we can better serve Him in one accord, just as we were originally designed. God declares, *"At that time I will change the speech of the people to a pure speech, that all of them may call upon the name of the LORD and serve him with one accord"* (Zeph. 3:9, ESV).

Having been conformed to the image of Christ in our thinking and our behavior, we as God's people will finally be able to fulfill our original task of stewarding God's creation as God's faithful imagers. Some will even be honored with stewarding humanity as members of God's redeemed human government. Regardless, each of us will possess a national identity and will have a meaningful role in ruling over God's creation in community forever.

Part 2

AMERICA'S WAR WITH GOD

CHAPTER 8

NO LONGER A CHRISTIAN NATION

Increasingly, America is rejecting its rich Christian heritage, its governing principles rooted in the Bible, and its Judeo-Christian belief in absolute truth and morality. Surveys indicate that only 6% of American adults possess a basic Christian worldview about things like God's attributes, the accuracy of the Bible, and salvation.[8, 9] Worse yet, the trend line is quickly declining:

- Americans over 50 (9%)
- Americans in their 30s and 40s (5%)
- Americans 18–29 (2%)[10]

Even among professing Christians, a basic biblical worldview is becoming increasingly rare:

- Evangelicals (21%)
- Pentecostals (16%)
- Mainline Protestants (8%)
- Catholics (1%)[11]

Given these figures, perhaps it is not surprising to discover that most professing Christians no longer adhere to the teachings of Jesus:

- Half of all professing Christians believe casual sex is okay: Catholic (62%), mainline protestants (54%), evangelicals (36%).[12, 13]
- 73% of pastors believe adultery shouldn't disqualify clergy from ministry.[14, 15]
- The majority of professing Christians believe abortion should be legal in all or most cases: Black Protestants (64%), white Protestants (63%), Catholics (55%), Evangelicals (21%).[16]
- 54% of Evangelicals believe religious belief is a matter of personal opinion, not objective truth.[17]
- 60% of professing born again Christians believe Muhammad, Buddha, and Jesus all taught valid paths to God.[18]

Only a small fraction of the 70% of Americans who identify as Christian are faithful followers of Jesus. It appears then-senator and presidential candidate Barack Obama was correct when he announced in 2006, "Whatever we once were, we are no longer a Christian nation—at least, not just. We are also a Jewish nation, a Muslim nation, a Buddhist nation, and a Hindu nation, and a nation of nonbelievers."[19, 20] This sentiment has been echoed by Christian leaders[21] and repeatedly championed in our national media with such headlines as:

- "The End of Christian America"[22] (*Newsweek*)

- "A Nation of Christians Is Not a Christian Nation"[23] (*New York Times*)
- "Why We Can Now Declare the End of 'Christian America'"[24] (*Washington Post*)
- "White Christian America Ended in the 2010s"[25] (*NBC News*)

Throughout America, the God of the Bible has been systematically removed from our government, our education system, our public arenas, our entertainment, and now from our worldview. Those vestiges of deity which remain in our culture have been largely reimagined to comport with otherwise conflicting worldviews. In practice, we have reimagined God to be one who submits to our American culture and lifestyle, not the other way around.

Although painful for many in the church to accept, the data reveals that America remains religious but is no longer governed by Christian principles. Most Americans remain happy to believe in God, but we are not willing to submit to Him because we have discovered a more attractive alternative—one that offers all the same spiritual benefits without the responsibility, effort, or accountability. As such, America has become a post-Christian society.

CHAPTER 9

A NATION IN REBELLION

Ironically, Americans are among the most anxious and least happy people in the world, despite being obsessed with personal happiness.[26, 27] Our relentless pursuit of pleasure has produced a culture defined by materialism, selfishness, pride, immorality, anger, retribution, and increasing lawlessness. Indeed, our quest to cast aside all moral restraints in pursuit of hedonistic euphoria has only unleashed societal chaos.

Despite the increasing difficulties that have ensued, our society refuses to turn back to God. Much like the ancient Israelites, we are a rebellious people who have chosen to ignore God's instructions and to stiffen our necks in response to His correction (Deut. 31:26–27; Jer. 17:23). Far from changing course, we have doubled down in our efforts:

- Our judiciary rules in opposition to God's law; our Congress legislates in opposition to God's commands; our educational system undermines

God's truth, and our entertainment industry regularly celebrates what God condemns.

- Our national media goes out of its way to excuse and protect nearly every expression of profanity, obscenity, and godless rebellious thinking expressed through social media, activism, art, and entertainment.
- Magazines, movies, television, and streaming shows promote premarital sex, adultery, polyamory, homosexuality, transgenderism, and even bestiality.[28]
- Unwilling to promote abstinence, our nation provides condoms to students as young as ten[29] and vaccinations against sexually transmitted diseases to 11-year-olds.[30]
- New York legislators offered a standing ovation after legalizing abortion up to the point of birth.[31] Worse yet, United States legislators refuse to protect babies born alive after failed abortions.[32]
- We have legalized, celebrated, and championed homosexuality and transgenderism—practices portrayed in the Bible as the most flagrant acts of rebellion against God and His created design and purpose for human relationships.
- Drag queen story hours are regular occurrences in libraries throughout our nation.[33, 34]
- We've legalized assisted suicide in numerous states.[35]

- Our state governments incentivize gambling, smoking, drinking, and drug use. The majority of states now offer needle exchange programs[36] to drug addicts, and some go so far as to provide safe spaces for injecting heroin.[37]

Having chosen a path of rebellion, our nation finds itself on a perilous trajectory. Our cultural pursuits are at odds with God. As such, we are headed for an inevitable conflict with our Creator if we do not change course.

CHAPTER 10

POISED FOR JUDGMENT

God judges rebellion and national disobedience by withholding His blessing and permitting times of nationwide difficulty and turmoil. Fundamentally, every nation is offered the same choice given to Israel: Choose God and receive blessing, or disobey God and be cursed (Deut. 11:26–28). God's heart is to bless nations, but rebellion provokes God to replace blessing with judgment.

Every nation charts its own path. God warns:

If I announce that a certain nation or kingdom is to be uprooted, torn down, and destroyed, but then that nation renounces its evil ways, I will not destroy it as I had planned. And if I announce that I will plant and build up a certain nation or kingdom, but then that nation turns to evil and refuses to obey me, I will not bless it as I said I would (Jer. 18:7–10).

The Bible is filled with accounts of God's judgment against nations (Eze. 25–26; Amos 1–2). When we consider the specific sins identified in these examples, it begs the question, "Is America poised for judgment?" Indeed, the very sins that provoked God to act in the past are often the defining elements of our modern American culture:

- Pride and arrogance (Amos 4:8; Obad. 1:2–4)
- Spiritual complacency and waywardness (Jer. 19:3–6; Amos6:1–7)
- Violence (Obad. 1:10; Nah. 3:1, 5)
- Culture of lies (Isa. 59:3–4, 13–18; Micah 6:12–13)
- Sexual immorality (Lev. 18:6–25; Amos 2:6–7)
- Corruption and injustice (Jer. 6:13, 19; Micah 6:11, 13)
- Oppression (Micah 2:2–3, 8–9; Zech. 7:10–11, 14)
- Promoting evil (Jer. 23:14–15; Micah 2:1–3)

America regularly celebrates and flaunts every one of these transgressions. The permeation of these sins into our culture is systemic, making a radical change necessary. We cannot continue indefinitely along this path without inciting a response from God.

CHAPTER 11

FROM DISCIPLINE TO DESTRUCTION

God's judgment often comes in two phases. The first phase is a corrective judgment in which God lifts His hand of blessing and protection, permitting a nation to experience the destructive consequences of sin. Pastor John MacArthur has referred to this as the wrath of abandonment.[38] It is designed to alert a nation to its need to repent. For instance, God judged the nation of Israel by selectively sending rain to some cities and not to others, by a lack of food and water, poor harvests, blight and mildew, locusts, disease, and military casualties; yet the people refused to repent and return to God (Amos 4:6–10).

A corrective judgment is disciplinary in nature. Like any corrective act, it may involve a time of great difficulty because it may require something extreme to capture the attention of the people. Nevertheless, some nations persist in their rebellion. Despite the severity of God's judgment against the Israelites, they failed to realize that they were a nation under judgment. Perhaps this is because God used natural means to accomplish His purposes. As such, the Israelites may have dismissed God's warning signals of famine, drought, disease, etc. as natural events. Regardless, their waywardness resulted in the second phase of God's judgment.

The second phase is a severe judgment. This often involves something designed to trouble a nation at a fundamental level. It is designed to shake a nation hard enough to compel the people to release the idols to which they are clinging. This usually results in the nation either letting go of its idols or falling alongside them, in which case, the nation may be destroyed by God. In the case of Israel, God eventually cast the Israelites out of their land, some of them even being taken away by fishhooks into captivity (Amos 4:2–3). Israel was ultimately made to confront its God as an adversary because it refused to respond to God's corrective judgment: *"Therefore, I will bring upon you all the disasters I have announced. Prepare to meet your God in judgment, you people of Israel!"* (Amos 4:12).

An argument can be made that America is presently experiencing God's corrective judgment. Certainly, we have experienced similar conditions to that of the Israelites when they were judged. Since the turn of the millennium, America has experienced the devastating attacks of 9-11, Hurricane Katrina, a plethora of mass shootings, soaring national debt, tumultuous race riots, the COVID-19 pandemic, a mental health epidemic, and more. If we refuse to draw near to God in our response, then we too may be made to confront God as an adversary. And if we do nothing to change our current trajectory, then America's discipline will eventually turn to destruction.

CHAPTER 12

POINT OF NO RETURN

It is possible for a nation in rebellion to reach a point of no return, securing an inevitable transition from God's discipline to destruction. When this point is reached, the nation cannot be spared the severity of God's judgment, even by the intercessory prayers of the righteous (Jer. 15:1–4). Ezekiel prophesies:

> *Then this message came to me from the* LORD*: "Son of man, suppose the people of a country were to sin against me, and I lifted my fist to crush them, cutting off their food supply and sending a famine to destroy both people and animals. ... Or suppose I were to send wild animals to invade the country, kill the people, and make the land too desolate and dangerous to pass through. ... Or suppose I were to bring war against the land, and I sent enemy armies to destroy both people and animals. ... Or suppose I were to pour out my fury by sending an epidemic into the land, and the disease killed people and animals alike. As surely as I live, says the Sovereign* LORD*, even if Noah,*

Daniel, and Job were there, they wouldn't be able to save their own sons or daughters. They alone would be saved by their righteousness" (Eze. 14:12–13, 15, 17, 19–20).

We find an example of this in Nahum's prophecy against Nineveh, the capitol of the Assyrian empire. Because of Nineveh's wickedness, judgment would come, and there would be no easing the nation's hurt (Nah. 3:1–19). Likewise, the prophet Jeremiah makes similar declarations against Judah and Israel (Jer. 10:18–19; 30:11–12).

The prophet Nahum questions Nineveh, *"Why are you scheming against the LORD? He will destroy you with one blow; he won't need to strike twice! His enemies tangled like thornbushes and staggering like drunks, will be burned up like dry stubble in a field. Who is this wicked counselor of yours who plots evil against the LORD?"* (Nah. 1:9–11). It is not possible to know the extent of God's patience in the face of evil, but it appears the point of no return may occur when a nation's waywardness is transformed into a persistent opposition of God—into an outright war against God (Isa. 59:11–14; Jer. 11:9–11).

It seems there is a difference between ignoring God's instruction and actively opposing it. This should give us pause, considering that America is enshrining its rebellion within its laws—permitting and encouraging its citizens to celebrate and champion evil. Increasingly, America is flaunting its disregard for God—aggressively parading it as a declaration of war against God Himself.

CHAPTER 13

REJECTING GOD'S PROPHETS

Prophets declare God's Word even when it is not welcome. When God sent national warnings to Judah, the people rejected and mocked the prophets:

> *Zedekiah did what was evil in the sight of the LORD his God, and he refused to humble himself when the prophet Jeremiah spoke to him directly from the LORD. ... Likewise, all the leaders of the priests and the people became more and more unfaithful. They followed all the pagan practices of the surrounding nations, desecrating the Temple of the LORD that had been consecrated in Jerusalem.*
>
> *The LORD, the God of their ancestors, repeatedly sent his prophets to warn them, for he had compassion on his people and his Temple.* ***But the people mocked these messengers of God and despised their words. They scoffed at the prophets*** *until the LORD'S anger could no longer be restrained and nothing could be done* (2 Chron. 36:12, 14–16, emphasis added).

Confronted with God's word, the people sought to silence God's messengers: *"'Don't say such things,' the people respond. 'Don't prophesy like that. Such disasters will never come our way!'"* (Micah 2:6). God, however, condemned their denial: *"Should you talk that way, O family of Israel? Will the LORD'S Spirit have patience with such behavior? If you would do what is right, you would find my words comforting. Yet to this very hour my people rise against me like an enemy!"* (Micah 2:7–8).

Seeking comfort but refusing to change their behavior, the people turned to other "prophets" who would tell them what they wanted to hear. However, God warned the people:

> *"Do not listen to these prophets when they prophesy to you, filling you with futile hopes. They are making up everything they say. They do not speak for the LORD! They keep saying to those who despise my word, 'Don't worry! The LORD says you will have peace!' And to those who stubbornly follow their own desires, they say, 'No harm will come your way!' Have any of these prophets been in the LORD'S presence to hear what he is really saying? Has even one of them cared enough to listen? Look! The LORD'S anger bursts out like a storm, a whirlwind that swirls down on the heads of the wicked. The anger of the LORD will not diminish until it has finished all he has planned"* (Jer. 23:16–20).

Eventually, Judah was conquered by the Babylonians, just as the prophets had warned (2 Chron. 36:17–21). No amount of denial, mockery, or effort to cancel and censor the prophets' message could change the nation's plight.

Only a radical change of behavior rooted in repentance could have prevented judgment (2 Chron. 7:14; Jer. 18:7–8). As Americans, we would do well to heed the example of Judah, lest we suffer the same fate.

CHAPTER 14

A NATION IN DENIAL

Judgment warnings are never welcome. When God sent prophetic warnings to Judah, the people rejected and mocked God's true prophets in favor of those "prophets" who told them what they hoped to hear. However, these prophets were liars:

> *Then I said, "O Sovereign LORD, their prophets are telling them, 'All is well—no war or famine will come. The LORD will surely send you peace.'"*
>
> *Then the LORD said, "These prophets are telling lies in my name. I did not send them or tell them to speak. I did not give them any messages. They prophesy of visions and revelations they have never seen or heard. They speak foolishness made up in their own lying hearts. Therefore, this is what the LORD says: I will punish these lying prophets, for they have spoken in my name even though I never sent them. They say that no war or famine will come, but they themselves will die by war and famine! As for the people to whom they prophesy—their bodies will*

be thrown out into the streets of Jerusalem, victims of famine and war. There will be no one left to bury them. Husbands, wives, sons, and daughters—all will be gone. For I will pour out their wickedness on them" (Jer. 14:13–16).

Not everyone who claims to speak for God can be trusted. Religious leaders who ignore sinful behavior and refuse to call people to repentance should be suspect—particularly if they promise blessing. The prophets' primary role in Scripture was to identify sin and to call people to repentance. Any comfort afforded by prophets was usually to allay the inevitable sense of hopelessness following the prophet's warning about the dire consequences of continued rebellion.

It is troubling how frequently today's Christian leaders in America "prophetically" declare God's favor upon our nation. Revival, prosperity, comfort, and blessing are readily promised without ever a mention of sin or a call to national repentance as a prerequisite for such divine favor. Such assurances defy God's written word: *"If I announce that I will plant and build up a certain nation or kingdom, but then that nation turns to evil and refuses to obey me, I will not bless it as I said I would"* (Jer. 18:9–10).

Rebellion results in judgment, not blessing. It is futile for us to hold out hope that God will miraculously transform our country when even our religious leaders are afraid to confront sin and to call people to repentance. Perhaps it is time we stop tickling our ears with vain assurances and face the reality of our situation. We are a nation at war with God, thus making us a nation poised for judgment unless we humbly renounce our sin and draw near to Him.

CHAPTER 15

REAPING THE WHIRLWIND

Having sown the wind for generations, is America now reaping the whirlwind? Our institutions are in chaos; our youth are in bondage; our churches are in decline; our government is in turmoil, and our foreign policy is in retreat. Moreover, our nation is experiencing astronomical debt, disease, anxiety, sexual confusion, agricultural calamity, and increasing foreign influence. These are the same corrective judgments God promised to use to draw Israel's heart back to Himself (Deut. 28:15–48):

- Curses, confusion, and frustration in the peoples' endeavors (v. 20)
- Disease and illness (vv. 21–22, 27–28, 35)
- Poor harvests, famine, and drought (vv. 22–24, 38–42)
- Military defeats (v. 25)
- Anxiety (v. 28)
- Oppression and robbery (vv. 29–34)

- Ridicule and mockery by other nations (v. 37)
- Increased foreign influence (v. 43)
- Increased debt (v. 44)

How is it that our nation is perpetually frustrated in these same ways, regardless of which political party is in power? Perhaps the reason we cannot seem to resolve these problems is because they are the consequence of our national war with God. As such, the solution will never be found in government, the judiciary, or in social justice reforms. They may simply be the consequence of God gradually removing His hand of blessing and protection from our nation.

These issues provide a kind of litmus test to help nations evaluate their spiritual condition. Habitual patterns of national difficulty encourage us to question whether they may be symptomatic of a spiritual ailment. Even disease and natural disasters may have a supernatural origin (Eze. 14:12–20; Amos 4:6–11). Rather than dismiss such difficulty as ordinary, or as the result of poor political decisions, we ought to be discerning enough to recognize that God may be attempting to capture our collective attention, hoping that we will respond in humility and once again draw near to Him.

This is illustrated in God's lament over Israel:

What sorrow awaits rebellious, polluted Jerusalem,
the city of violence and crime!
No one can tell it anything;
it refuses all correction.
It does not trust in the LORD

or draw near to its God.
Its leaders are like roaring lions
hunting for their victims.
Its judges are like ravenous wolves at evening time,
who by dawn have left no trace of their prey.
Its prophets are arrogant liars seeking their own gain.
Its priests defile the Temple by disobeying God's instructions.
But the LORD *is still there in the city,*
and he does no wrong.
Day by day he hands down justice,
and he does not fail.
But the wicked know no shame.

"I have wiped out many nations,
devastating their fortress walls and towers.
Their streets are now deserted;
their cities lie in silent ruin.
There are no survivors—
none at all.
I thought, 'Surely they will have reverence for me now!
Surely they will listen to my warnings.
Then I won't need to strike again,
destroying their homes.'
But no, they get up early
To continue their evil deeds.
Therefore, be patient," says the LORD.
"Soon I will stand and accuse these evil nations" (Zeph. 3:1–8a).

Let us draw near to God in repentance while there remains time (2 Chron. 7:13–14; James 4:4–10).

CHAPTER 16

IS IT TOO LATE?

Merciful and patient as God may be, there is a limit to His tolerance of sin. Severe judgment awaits those nations that ignore God's corrective judgments. Nations that, like rebellious Israel, arrogantly respond to corrective judgment by declaring, "'*We will replace the broken bricks of our ruins with finished stone, and replant the felled sycamore-fig trees with cedars*'" (Isa. 9:10), compel God to dispense ever greater measures of judgment until, finally, all that remains is final destruction.

When exactly a nation's stubbornness transitions its judgment from discipline to destruction is never specified in God's Word. Indeed, prophetic warnings often preceded God's judgment by decades—and even generations—granting ample opportunity for repentance. Israel fell to Assyria about 40 years after Amos' declaration (Amos 7); Assyria's capital city fell to the Babylonians and Medes around 50 years after Nahum's prophecy (Nah. 1–3), and Babylon fell to the Medo-Persians 66 years after Habakkuk's warning (Hab. 2:4–20). Undoubtedly, God's prophets believed that severe judgment upon these nations was imminent—and likely unavoidable. However, God bestowed a prolonged season of mercy before sending His destruction.

Likewise, we would rightly assume that the evil capital city of Assyria had exhausted God's mercy when reading the prophet Jonah's warning: *"Forty days from now Nineveh will be destroyed!"* (Jonah 3:4). Nevertheless, God responded to the city's humble repentance by extending mercy for nearly 150 years. We simply have no way of knowing when it is too late for a nation to stave off God's destructive judgment.

Similarly, we have no way of knowing how long our national season of mercy will last. As such, we should not preach imminent destruction, but neither should we presume God's continued mercy. Instead, we ought to faithfully uphold righteousness where we have influence and to intercede on behalf of our nation, like Habakkuk, who pleaded with God, *"In your anger, remember your mercy"* (Hab. 3:2). As we do, let us resist becoming fatalistic in our thinking as we boldly proclaim the heart of God: Love God, obey Him, and firmly commit to Him in everything so that we might prosper (Deut. 30:20).

CHAPTER 17

WHAT CAN WE DO?

Far from encouraging a fatalistic mindset, 2 Chronicles 7:13–14 provides God's people with an action plan for aligning our hearts with the heart of God in times of crisis: "*'At times I might shut up the heavens so that no rain falls, or command grasshoppers to devour your crops, or send plagues among you. Then if my people who are called by my name will humble themselves and pray and seek my face and turn from their wicked ways, I will hear from heaven and will forgive their sins and restore their land.'*"

- **Humble ourselves** – We can submit our ambitions, our reputations, our possessions, and our emotions to God as the sovereign ruler.

- **Repent** – We can examine our own hearts and repent of any sin we may be harboring.

- **Renounce evil** – We can assess our national culture with the intent of separating ourselves from any cultural mindset that contravenes God's moral commands.

- **Prayerfully seek God** – We can seek God's will for our lives and for our nation.

- **Engage culture** – Implicit in all this is that we should also challenge those around us to follow these steps of evaluation, repentance, and submission.

- **Trust God's heart** – We can fall to our knees to intercede for mercy upon our nation, asking that God will grant us more time to influence those around us with the transforming power of the gospel. We can trust that God's heart is not to judge but to restore a righteous relationship with His people and ask that He will grant us more opportunity to accomplish this.

If enough citizens internalize 2 Chronicles 7:13–14, perhaps God will relent, just as He did toward Nineveh: *"When God saw what they did, how they turned from their evil way, God relented of the disaster that he had said he would do to them, and he did not do it"* (Jonah 3:10, ESV).

CHAPTER 18

GOD'S SOLUTION

The national difficulties mentioned in 2 Chronicles 7:13 are the plagues that Moses warned would befall Israel if the nation neglected God. Moses anticipated and warned against a time when Israel's peace and prosperity would lead to spiritual complacency:

> *Beware that in your plenty you do not forget the* LORD *your God and disobey his commands, regulations, and decrees that I am giving you today. For when you have become full and prosperous and have built fine homes to live in, and when your flocks and herds have become large and your silver and gold have multiplied along with everything else, be careful! Do not become proud at that time and forget the* LORD *your God ... I assure you of this: If you ever forget the* LORD *your God and follow other gods, worshipping and bowing to them, you will certainly be destroyed* (Deut. 8:11b–14a, 19).

Importantly, Moses' solution was fundamentally the same as God's instruction in 2 Chronicles 7:13–14: "*I command you this day to love the LORD your God and to keep his commands, decrees, and regulations by walking in his ways. If you do this, you will live and multiply, and the LORD your God will bless you and the land you are about to enter and occupy"* (Deut. 30:16).

God's solution to our problems remains the same today. His solution is consistently sprawled across the pages of Scripture from beginning to end: Stop rebelling. God told Cain in the first pages of the Old Testament, *"You will be accepted if you do what is right. But if you refuse to do what is right, then watch out!"* (Gen. 4:7a). And Jesus announced in the New Testament, *"'You must love the LORD your God with all your heart, all your soul, and all your mind'"* (Matt. 22:37).

What we can do when confronted with the consequences of our rebellion is stop rebelling. We can replace our defiance with obedience. In short, we can love God and obey Him.

CHAPTER 19

WE MUST OWN THIS WAR

We the people own this war against God. Tempting as it may be to shift responsibility to our national leaders, we cannot forget that our leadership does only what we permit. Unfortunately, we have permitted a national assault against God.

America is exceptional because it is a nation founded upon biblical principles. When we fight for these values to be upheld and preserved, we are fighting to see God's truth upheld and preserved within our nation. As such, there is a place and a need for vigilant Christian citizens to actively engage in politics. However, the value of such politics rests in seeing these biblical principles realized. In other words, the solutions to our national difficulties must always be primarily spiritual, not merely political.

The strength of our American government has always rested upon its moral alignment with God. Indeed, founding father and former president John Adams warned that our Constitution was made only for a religious and moral people: "We have no Government armed with Power capable of contending with human Passions unbridled by morality and Religion. Avarice, Ambition, Revenge or Gallantry, would break the strongest Cords of our Constitution as a Whale goes through a Net. Our Constitution was made only for a moral and religious People. It is wholly inadequate to the government of any other."[39]

According to John Adams, it is not simply the Constitution we must fervently protect if we wish to keep America strong, nor is it a political philosophy. It is the morality of America's citizenry, shepherded by the church, that must be safeguarded. As goes the church, so goes the nation.

When the American church chooses to remain silent on political and culturally controversial matters that are fundamentally moral, is it any wonder how our nation has lost respect for God's opinion regarding life's most significant issues? When pastors are more afraid of offending people than of offending God, is it any wonder how our nation has made tolerance a greater virtue than righteousness? When God's people are more committed to the American Dream than they are to the Great Commission, is it any wonder how our nation has become obsessively materialistic?

As Martin Luther King Jr. famously preached, "The church must be reminded that it is not the master or the servant of the state, but rather the conscience of the state. It must be the guide and the critic of the state, and never its tool. If the church does not recapture its prophetic zeal, it will become an irrelevant social club without moral or spiritual authority."[40] If we have any hope of resolving our national conflict with God, we, as the people of God, must own our role in this war.

CHAPTER 20

THIS IS OUR WAR TO SURRENDER

America's war with God began in our churches and in our households, not in our government. As such, the responsibility to surrender this war with God ultimately rests with each of us individually, not with our government leaders. Until we are willing to personally humble ourselves and to submit our own lives, households, churches, and communities to God's will, our nation will never relent of its revolt.

When will enough be enough? How much difficulty must we endure before we repent of our rebellion against God? It is time for us to stop pointing the finger of blame at the deficiencies of our national leadership, expecting change to come from the top. America has always been a nation of the people, by the people, and for the people. Change can come to the top, but only if it starts with us. As such, it is we the people who will determine the course of our nation and the outcome of this war with God.

One way or the other, God will win this war. Surrender is our best option. Our only alternative is to be defeated.

In His mercy, God is presently making the same appeal to each and every one of us that He made to Israel: *"Today I have given you the choice between life and death, between blessings and curses. ... Oh that you would choose life, so that you and your descendants might live! You can make this choice by loving the* LORD *your God, obeying him, and committing yourself firmly to him. This is the key to your life"* (Deut. 30:19–20a). The choice is ours. What will we choose?

Part 3

SOUNDING THE ALARM

CHAPTER 21

CLINGING TO HOPE

Apart from national repentance, America will be unable to avoid divine judgment. Discomforting as the thought may be, this is a good thing. It is important that God relent of the good He has planned for nations that do evil and rebel against His instructions. Without the incentive of pain and discomfort, we as humans rarely feel the need to change our behavior.

God says, *"If I announce that I will plant and build up a certain nation or kingdom, but then that nation turns to evil and refuses to obey me, I will not bless it as I said I would"* (Jer. 18:9–10). God knows that being in a right relationship with Himself is more important than temporary comfort and pleasure. It is considerably better to experience the difficulty of a national judgment that alerts us to the folly of our rebellion against God than it is to be permitted to traverse our rebellious path to its final destination of permanent separation from Him and the abundant life that God offers in His eternal kingdom (Rev. 20:11–15; 21:8, 23–27).

Difficult as it may be to appreciate, God's corrective judgments are a mercy. They are God's refusal to abandon His hope that a nation's citizenry will choose the blessings associated with God's kingdom over its cultural idols. These idols are the manifestation of a nation's rebellious ideology; however, when a nation refuses to relinquish its idols, God will eventually shake that nation hard enough to cause them to fall. This is God's severe judgment. In that moment, the people must choose whether to release their idols or to fall alongside them.

The experience of Israel illustrates this pattern. In Amos, God laments Israel's refusal to respond to His corrective judgments: *"'I destroyed some of your cities, as I destroyed Sodom and Gomorrah. Those of you who survived were like charred sticks pulled from a fire. But still you would not return to me,' says, the Lord"* (Amos 4:11). Consequently, God warns that He will shake the nation to the point of collapse:

> *Prepare to meet your God in judgment, you people of Israel! ... I, the Sovereign LORD, am watching this sinful nation of Israel. I will destroy it from the face of the earth. But I will never completely destroy the family of Israel, says the LORD. For I will give the command and will shake Israel along with the other nations as grain is shaken in a sieve, yet not one true kernel will be lost. But all the sinners will die by the sword—all those who say, "Nothing bad will happen to us"* (Amos 4:12b; 9:8–10).

This prophecy was fulfilled in 721 B.C. when Assyria conquered Israel. However, this was not God's intended will for Israel. He is not eager to destroy people and nations in judgment. Rather, God's desire is that we obey Him. According to Jeremiah 18:7, had Israel repented of its sin, God would have likely delayed judgment: *"If I announce that a certain nation or kingdom is to be uprooted, torn down, and destroyed, but then that nation renounces its evil ways, I will not destroy it as I had planned."*

God warned the Israelites to give them both opportunity and motivation to repent. When we declare God's warning, we join with Him in clinging to this same hope that people will be motivated to repent. As long as there remains opportunity to warn, there remains hope that a nation will relent of its rebellion and receive mercy. However, we deprive our nation of this opportunity if we are unwilling to sound the alarm.

CHAPTER 22

WHITEWASHED TOMBS

In America, not only have we increasingly failed to fulfill our divine mandate to draw the hearts of people back to God, but we have sown and cultivated seeds of the very behaviors that are provoking God to judge our nation. Rather than prioritize righteousness, Americans have championed sexual perversion over sexual purity, greed and materialism over generosity, narratives over truth, and a culture of death over a culture of life. Even within the church, we have often ignored these cultural issues from without while tacitly accepting them from within. Moreover, rather than model Jesus' humility, faithfulness to God's Word, and dependency upon the Holy Spirit, we ourselves have often displayed a spirit of pride and self-sufficiency. We have frequently shown ourselves to be lukewarm instead of living a surrendered, faith-filled life for Jesus, regardless of the cost.

Let us not deceive ourselves into believing we are more righteous than we truly are—like the religious leaders in the time of Jesus whose spiritual pride blinded them to the work God was accomplishing:

> *"What sorrow awaits you teachers of religious law and you Pharisees. Hypocrites! For you are like whitewashed tombs—beautiful on the outside but filled on the inside with dead people's bones and all sorts of impurity. Outwardly you look like righteous people, but inwardly your hearts are filled with hypocrisy and lawlessness"* (Matt. 23:27–28).

When God judged the nation of Israel for its rebellion, God's judgment fell also upon these religious leaders who were quick, throughout the gospels, to condemn the conduct of others (Matt. 23:36).

Before we critique other people's behavior and exhort them to repent, we ourselves must first determine what remains to be repented of in our own lives. Jesus cautions, *"How can you think of saying, 'Friend, let me help you get rid of that speck in your eye,' when you can't see past the log in your own eye? Hypocrite! First get rid of the log in your own eye; then you will see well enough to deal with the speck in your friend's eye"* (Luke 6:42).

Although we assent to Christ in our minds, we may not always assent to Him in our hearts. This partial allegiance may fool others, but it will not fool God, who is able to discern the motivations of our heart: *"People may be pure in their own eyes, but the LORD examines their motives"* (Prov. 16:2). Some of us have become comfortable living in a rebellious nation because a part of our heart has never relinquished all of our nation's cultural idols. However, the end result of such divided loyalty is still judgment. Indeed, this is the mentality God addresses in Revelation 18:4 when judging Babylon: "*'Come away from her, my people. Do not take part in her sins, or you will be punished with her.'*"

God requires total allegiance. When He shakes a nation to the point that its cultural idols fall, everyone still clinging to those idols will fall with them—regardless of whether they are numbered among the people of God. Therefore, it is incumbent upon us to evaluate our hearts to determine whether we have given God our full allegiance. Before we warn others of the consequences of living in continued rebellion, let us be certain to fully repent of our own refusal to obey God's instructions (1 John 1:9).

CHAPTER 23

BECOMING WATCHMEN

It would be unconscionable to watch a toddler's curious and lustful advances toward a hot stove without warning him of the dangers of touching his obsession. Similarly, it would be immoral to silently observe as a child chases his ball into a busy street, oblivious to danger. Even among adults, warnings are necessary and expected. Nobody should be permitted to handle a loaded gun for the first time without being warned of the consequences of mishandling the weapon. Neither should a doctor withhold his warning against ignoring treatment options. Although warnings are not always appreciated in the moment, our society expects responsible citizens to warn those who are being irresponsible. Likewise, we must warn others of the consequences of our continued rebellion to God's instructions.

So committed are we to protecting others in our society that we place upon ourselves an expectation not only to warn but to intervene, if necessary. Hospitals have sought legal recourse to provide reluctant patients the treatment they need, and guardians have often rushed to intercept children who are headed for danger. Why then would we assume, having been made aware of our nation's perilous trajectory, that we bear no responsibility to warn others about God's judgment? We have an obligation, after first ensuring that we ourselves are no longer living in rebellion, to warn others—and if necessary, to intervene in their lives—to protect them from disaster.

If we see calamity approaching but choose to remain silent, then we bear a portion of responsibility for whatever happens:

> *"When the watchman sees the enemy coming, he sounds the alarm to warn the people. Then if those who hear the alarm refuse to take action, it is their own fault if they die. They heard the alarm but ignored it, so the responsibility is theirs. If they had listened to the warning, they could have saved their lives. But if the watchman sees the enemy coming and doesn't sound the alarm to warn the people, he is responsible for their captivity. They will die in their sins, but I will hold the watchman responsible for their deaths"* (Eze. 33:3–6).

Likewise, if we see disaster coming, but if the urgency of our warning is not proportional to the threat, then we bear a portion of responsibility for whatever happens. After all, a watchman whose cry is not loud enough to wake the sleeping citizenry would be useless, despite having sounded some form of alarm.

Gentle exhortation to avoid the street is appropriate when a child is content to play in the yard, but a forceful warning is necessary when that same child is running toward the road. Similarly, our time for gentle exhortation in America is past. Our nation is careening along a perilous path, and we are unable to discern how much distance remains before it descends into disaster. Those of us who recognize our predicament must become our nation's watchmen and fervently sound an alarm.

CHAPTER 24

HOW TO SOUND THE ALARM

Understanding God's purpose for nations and America's war with God should produce in us a yearning to reach others before it is too late with a warning about the consequences of our nation's perilous trajectory. Our concern provokes us to become forerunners of God's judgment who feel compelled to sound the alarm because we reserve hope that a change of mindset and behavior can stave-off destruction and restore our relationship with God. As such, our warning is not a decree of fated disaster. Instead, our warning is a call to action that emphasizes the consequences of inaction. But how do we do this?

How we warn others must be tailored to both our audience and our own personality. Nonetheless, there is a key Bible passage that ought to serve as the lynchpin in any approach:

> *If I [God] announce that a certain nation or kingdom is to be uprooted, torn down, and destroyed, but then that nation renounces its evil ways, I will not destroy*

> *it as I had planned. And if I announce that I will plant and build up a certain nation or kingdom, but then that nation turns to evil and refuses to obey me, I will not bless it as I said I would* (Jer. 18:7–10).

This is God's standard for evaluating nations and for determining their future. Far from being fated to a particular destiny, we the people are given an opportunity to determine our nation's course. Throughout the Bible, this statement of God's is never revoked or amended. God has always weighed nations according to their faithfulness to Him, and He continues to weigh nations by this standard today.

God does not desire to judge nations; He desires to bless nations, and His hope is that we will respond to the difficulty of judgment by drawing near to Him in repentance. God's Word assures us, "*Come close to God, and God will come close to you. Wash your hands, you sinners; purify your hearts, for your loyalty is divided between God and the world*" (James 4:8). This principle holds true not only for individuals, but also for nations. God tells Solomon:

> "*At times I might shut up the heavens so that no rain falls, or command grasshoppers to devour your crops, or send plagues among you. Then if my people who are called by my name will humble themselves and pray and seek my face and turn from their wicked ways, I will hear from heaven and will forgive their sins and restore their land*" (2 Chron. 7:13–14).

Our warnings should reflect both the severity of God's judgment against sinful behavior and God's heart for restoration. Likewise, our warnings should hold out the hope that, if enough citizens internalize 2 Chronicles 7:13–14, God will relent, just as He did toward Nineveh: *"When God saw what they did, how they turned from their evil way, God relented of the disaster that he had said he would do to them, and he did not do it"* (Jonah 3:10, ESV). God responded to Nineveh's humble repentance by extending mercy for nearly 150 years.

Given the stakes, we are compelled to warn others. However we choose to do this, our warning should not be made with a spirit of fear, judgmentalism, or cynicism, but with a spirit that balances our grief concerning national waywardness with hope. This is the heart of a forerunner.

Part 4

MAKING A DIFFERENCE

CHAPTER 25

WHAT IS OUR CONCERN?

Confronted with the reality that America is on a perilous trajectory in need of Christians who will sound the alarm, each of us has a decision to make: Are we willing to become forerunners of God's judgment in the hope of making a difference in our nation? Of course, this is far too broad and abstract a question to meaningfully answer, so let's make it practical by first breaking down what we mean when we say we want to make a difference. Let's begin with what concerns us. After all, before we can determine whether we want to make a difference, we ought to know whether we are satisfied with the way things are now.

About what are we concerned? Likely, each of us could readily provide a lengthy list: Rampant sexual immorality and confusion, the humanistic indoctrination of our children, society's lack of respect and civility, widespread corruption, injustice, partisan politics, economic uncertainty, porous borders, the loss of traditional values, the denial of objective truth, attacks against religious liberty, the ineffectiveness of the church, and so much more. Certainly, there are plenty of issues about which to worry, but these are merely symptomatic of a greater problem. When we cut to the chase, our primary concern for America ought to be over our nation's increasing disregard for its prime directive: To draw the hearts of people back to God.

America exists to draw people to God. This sense of purpose is not a pursuit of spiritual meaning to justify our patriotism. Rather, it is what God's Word tells us: *"From one man [God] created all the nations throughout the whole earth. He decided beforehand when they should rise and fall, and he determined their boundaries. His purpose was for the nations to seek after God and perhaps feel their way toward him and find him—though he is not far from any one of us"* (Acts 17:26–27). God's purpose for nations is to encourage a pursuit of God.

Certainly, there have been seasons in our history when we, as a nation, glorified God. God has used America to draw people to Himself, and He continues to do so today. Indeed, America's esteem for religious liberty and freedom of speech affords us great opportunity to share the good news of the gospel and the truth of God's Word. Moreover, America is an affluent country, and many of us use our wealth to finance global mission projects.

On the other hand, we in America have been systematically removing God from our government, our educational system, our entertainment, and our way of life. "In God we trust" is becoming a national motto devoid of meaning as many of our most influential institutions now actively push people away from Him. Indeed, America has long been waging an escalating war against God.

One cannot help but ask the question, "If America is no longer accomplishing its divine purpose, then why should God continue to bless and preserve our nation?" How are we any different from the nation of Judah, whom God warned:

> *If I announce that I will plant and build up a certain nation or kingdom, but then that nation turns to evil and refuses to obey me, I will not bless it as I said I would. Therefore, Jeremiah, go warn all Judah and Jerusalem. Say to them, "This is what the LORD says: I am planning disaster for you instead of good. So turn from your evil ways, each of you, and do what is right"* (Jer. 18:9–11)?

Like Judah, America is on a perilous trajectory. As such, we cannot be satisfied with the status quo, but neither can we afford to become distracted by matters that ought to be secondary concerns. Instead, our greatest concern should be over our nation's increasing disregard for its divine purpose: To draw the hearts of people back to God.

CHAPTER 26

SILENCE OF THE LAMBS

The vast majority of Americans believe our nation's moral compass is pointed in the wrong direction. This sentiment is consistent across religious and political persuasions. Even seven in ten Americans who do not practice religion feel this way.[41] Not coincidentally, most Americans also believe being religious is unnecessary in living a moral life,[42] and their religion does not factor into their political identification.[43]

Somewhere along the line, God's people bought into the lie that Christians should not engage in politics—as if our beliefs should not influence how we live in community with others. It is argued that politics is a dirty business relating to the kingdom of the world, but Christians are called to be separated in holiness and to focus on the kingdom of God. Polling shows that most Americans want churches to stay out of politics—particularly during political elections; however, such thinking wrongly assumes that God has no interest in the way nations govern themselves.[44] Moreover, by removing ourselves from the conversation, we, as God's people, forfeit our opportunity to hold culture accountable to God's Word and to keep evil at bay.

Martin Luther King Jr. preached that it is the church that ought to serve as the conscience of the nation.[45] If our nation's moral compass is misaligned, it is our fault. We should expect that, if God's people remain silent, our nation will naturally veer into immorality. Like a frog in a kettle, Americans will instinctively adapt to accommodate increasing rebellion and evil, oblivious to our true peril.

As an illustration, consider the matter of abortion. Within a generation, what was once touted as "safe, legal, and rare" became "shout your abortion."[46] Moreover, our nation's moral depravity regarding the lives of our most innocent continues to escalate. God's people largely remained silent when the "Born-Alive Survivors Protection Act" failed to pass the U.S. Senate. The bill sought to provide safeguards for newborns in the 19 states without legal protections for children born alive after a failed abortion[47] by requiring that health care providers offer any such baby the same level of medical care they would give to any other infant at the same gestational age.[48] Only three years later, some states took the matter to a whole new level by introducing legislation that would decriminalize some forms of infanticide.[49, 50]

Abortion may be a political issue, but it is fundamentally a moral matter, and it is foolish to believe that God does not want His representatives to speak into the issue. Indeed, our failure to do so has only permitted the immorality of murdering unborn babies to escalate into the immorality of murdering newborn babies. If God's people continue to remain silent, the acceptable parameters of murder will only expand. This is particularly significant now that the Supreme Court has returned the issue of abortion to each state to determine if and when it is acceptable to terminate human life.

How can a nation ever hope to draw the hearts of people back to God if God's people refuse to share His heart on practical life issues and to hold culture to account? This does not mean that we should speak into every political issue or become obsessed with those civic matters that have no eternal consequence. Nonetheless, there are plenty of cultural issues that are fundamentally moral matters. These are the issues that will either draw a nation's heart toward God or drive a wedge of hostility between the people and God. As such, we should be terribly concerned about the silence of God's people when it comes to moral matters in our culture.

CHAPTER 27

EMBRACING OUR MESSAGE

A popular, yet dangerous, myth maintains that God wants His people to be known by what they are for, not what they are against. After all, Jesus told His disciples, *"By this all people will know that you are my disciples, if you have love for one another"* (John 13:35, ESV). Therefore, it is argued that Christians should be silent on divisive cultural issues and the consequences of immorality. Instead, we should show love to others by being willing to overlook their sinful behavior as we proclaim the love, mercy, forgiveness, and patience of God. In an article titled "Should Christians Not Be Known for What They Are Against?" Pastor Eric Davis provides an outstanding rebuke of this popular notion.[51] What follows are highlights from his article.

Such sentiments produce compelling memes and attractive sermons that sound noble, but they are far from biblical. Eight of God's ten commandments involved an explicit instruction to be against something (Exo. 20). As the people of God, Israel was expected to be a holy people to the nations, meaning that they were to be known for their differences. Indeed, entire chapters of commandments saying that the people "must not" and should "never" begin with the prefaces, *"Since you are the people of the Lord your God,"* and, *"You have been set apart as holy to the LORD your God, and he has chosen you from all the nations of the earth to be his own special treasure"* (Deut. 14:1a, 2a).

Likewise, the apostle Paul indicates, in Ephesians, that God's people should be against living like unbelievers (4:17–22); falsehood (4:25); stealing (4:28); unwholesome speech (4:29); grieving the Holy Spirit (4:30); bitterness, wrath, anger, clamor, and slander (4:31); unforgiveness (4:32); sexual immorality, impurity, and greed (5:2); filthiness, foolish talk, and crude joking (5:4); and the works of darkness (5:11). Paul challenges Christians to expose evil and to oppose false doctrine (Eph. 5:11; 1 Tim. 1:3).

Many New Testament books were written specifically to refute and correct false teaching. Paul instructs the Corinthian church to be against self-aggrandizement (1 Cor. 1–2); self-ambition in ministry (1 Cor. 3–4); bragging (1 Cor. 4); refusing to carry out church discipline (1 Cor. 5); inter-Christian lawsuits and sexual immorality (1 Cor. 6); unbiblical divorce and aimless singleness (1 Cor. 7); self-centeredness in liberties (1 Cor. 8–9); and confusion in corporate worship (1 Cor. 14). Galatians is written to let everyone know that God's people are to be against the idea that anyone can be acceptable before God apart from justification by faith alone, in Christ alone, and Colossians opposes teachings that Jesus was less than fully God and truly human.

At the end of his ministry, Peter devotes an entire chapter to opposing false teachers and their doctrines (2 Pet. 2). Likewise, Jude begins his letter with the explanation:

> *Dear friends, I had been eagerly planning to write to you about the salvation we all share. But now I find that I must write about something else, urging you to defend the faith that God has entrusted once for all time to his holy people. I say this because some ungodly people have wormed their way into your churches, saying that God's marvelous grace allows us to live immoral lives. The condemnation of such people was recorded long ago, for they have denied our only Master and Lord, Jesus Christ* (Jude 1:3–4).

Even Jesus was hated by many because of what He was known for being against. Jesus opposed self-aggrandizing attitudes that could not receive correction, were sensitive to reproof, and were unwilling to confront sin. Often, this placed Jesus in direct opposition to the religious leaders of His day (Matt. 21:45–46; 23:1–36; Luke 11:45–46).

We cannot be known by what we are *for* without also being known by what we are *against*. We cannot truly love people if we are unwilling to oppose and punish those who rape and murder. We cannot value health if we are not opposed to disease and lifestyle habits that diminish our health. We cannot cherish being created in the image of God if we are not opposed to racism and prejudice. And we cannot champion morality if we are willing to turn a blind eye to rampant immorality. Being for something necessitates that we also be against something else. They are two sides of the same coin, which may be the reason the Bible never commands us to be known by either what we are for or against. Instead, God's goal for His people is broader: *"Whatever you do, do it all for the glory of God"* (1 Cor. 10:31b). As King Solomon concluded, God expects us to *"fear God and keep his commandments, for this is the whole duty of man"* (Ecc. 12:13b, ESV). Sometimes this means championing something, and sometimes it means opposing something.

God does not devote huge portions of His Word to identifying what He opposes and to warning of the consequences of ignoring His instructions for no purpose. As God's representatives, God expects us to share these truths with others. Therefore, we cannot be silent on moral issues, and we cannot neglect to warn others of the personal and national consequences of continued sinful rebellion to His instructions.

CHAPTER 28

WHAT DO WE HOPE TO CHANGE?

Having identified our primary concerns as being our nation's failure to accomplish its divine purpose of drawing the hearts of people back to God and the silence of God's people regarding moral matters in our culture, what is it we hope to change as forerunners? Ultimately, we desire to see our nation repent and become obedient to God. As such, it seems natural that we should focus our efforts on changing the beliefs and behavior of Americans. Should we then seek to address our concerns by altering our nation's laws? In other words, should we primarily focus on changing the culture via legislation?

Although we often speak of "the culture" in monolithic terms, reality is far more complicated. There isn't any one culture that defines America—or even the majority of America today. Our nation consists of several divergent cultures. It seems that each generation has developed its own set of customs and values, which are often a repudiation of the prior generation. The culture of the Greatest

Generation is distinct from that of the Baby-Boomers. In fact, the Baby-Boomers defined entire decades by the rejection of their parents' customs and values. Likewise, to some degree, Generation X rejected much of their parents' culture—as have Generation Y (the Millennials) and, it appears from our limited data, Generation Z. In all honesty, we have at least five very distinct generations living together, resulting in an all-out culture war.

The solution to the culture war, for many Christians, has been a return to the mindset of a previous generation. However, in their heyday, every generation's dominant culture progressed our nation further along the same perilous path. Even if we were to return to the cultural mindset of the Greatest Generation, we would still be a nation that is becoming increasingly immoral while God's people become increasingly silent. Granted, it may be an improvement from what we are experiencing today, but it still wouldn't be sufficient to truly address our primary concerns because people's hearts would remain unmoved.

Other Christians have found it easier to enforce morality via legislation than to persuade people to submit their will to God. Certainly, we hope that our involvement in political grassroot movements will result in positive national change, but success in these areas is unlikely to produce the transformative change we truly desire. Indeed, Christians have already tried this and failed.

In the 1980's, the Moral Majority movement witnessed great success in enacting new laws designed to preserve righteousness and to protect traditional values. Although there were many good things that came from this movement, we ultimately learned that changing a person's behavior without changing the heart is self-defeating. All it can do is delay the inevitable. So, while we can, and should, be involved in the legislative process, the difference we are seeking to make as forerunners cannot be exclusively legislative.

The way a person behaves is merely a manifestation of what that person believes. Likewise, how a nation behaves stems from what its citizenry believes. Ultimately, lasting and meaningful change requires that people alter the way they think, but it is difficult to influence the thinking of an entire nation if we do not have a national platform from which to speak. Whose thinking, then, should we target?

We can be far more influential if we will focus our efforts toward the people in our natural spheres of influence: Family, friends, co-workers, neighbors. These are people who already love and respect us. As such, they are much more likely to consider what we have to say. Likewise, they are far more likely to respond to what we have to say. Therefore, as forerunners, we hope to make a difference by prioritizing individuals, choosing to influence the nation by influencing the way the people in our own communities think about moral matters.

CHAPTER 29

THE TASK OF A FORERUNNER

Our ability to think and to make decisions have been fundamentally corrupted. As much as we may want to believe that humanity is naturally inclined to choose what is right and true, reality paints a far bleaker picture. God told the prophet Jeremiah, *"'The human heart is the most deceitful of all things, and desperately wicked. Who really knows how bad it is?'"* (Jer. 17:9). Likewise, the apostle Paul teaches, *"No one is truly wise; no one is seeking God. ... No one does good, not a single one"* (Rom. 3:11, 12b).

Left to ourselves, we consistently choose a self-destructive path that leads to divine judgment. Indeed, Paul notes that God's judgment against *"people who suppress the truth by their wickedness,"* even though *"they know the truth about God,"* was simply to *"abandon them to do whatever shameful things their hearts desired"* (Rom. 1:18–19, 24). Pastor John MacArthur calls this judgment God's wrath of abandonment.[52] This is when God steps aside and permits humanity to suffer the full consequences of their natural inclinations and poor decisions.

Truth be told, we must often be warned of the consequences of our decisions before we can think clearly—before we are willing to deny our passions and do what is right. Perhaps this is why, when establishing Israel as a nation for Himself, God provided a detailed description of the blessings *and the judgments* that would come upon the people according to how faithful they were to follow His instructions (Deut. 28). It is not sufficient to speak only about God's blessings. We must also warn people about the consequences of their continued rebellion against God's instructions. Only then will they be fully equipped to make an informed decision before it is too late.

John the Baptist serves as a model forerunner who went ahead of the Messiah, preparing the people to meet God. It was prophesied of John, *"It is he who will go as a forerunner before Him in the spirit and power of Elijah, to turn the hearts of the fathers back to the children, and the disobedient to the attitude of the righteous, so as to make ready a people prepared for the Lord"* (Luke 1:17, NASB, capitalizations removed). John accomplished this, not merely by proclaiming the arrival of the Messiah and His kingdom, but by warning of the consequences of meeting a holy God while still living in sinful rebellion to Him. As such, he preached a message of repentance for the forgiveness of sins (Mark 1:4) and warned, *"Even now the ax of God's judgment is poised, ready to sever the roots of the trees. Yes, every tree that does not produce good fruit will be chopped down and thrown into the fire"* (Luke 3:9).

If we truly wish to change the way people think about moral matters, then we must first change the way they think about the consequences of their decisions. However, we do not simply declare judgment. Rather, like John the Baptist, we call everyone to respond in faith by submitting themselves to God. Thus, we hope to change the way people live by extending to them God's invitation to bring their beliefs into alignment with His will and ways.

CHAPTER 30

WHAT ABOUT POLITICAL ACTIVISM?

Political activism is an important part of our patriotic duty, but as forerunners, our primary goal is not to change how the president thinks—or even the thinking of our political representatives. Rather, we seek to make a difference by changing the thinking of those with whom we already have influence, such as family members, friends, co-workers, and neighbors. We challenge them to reconsider what our nation is doing versus what it should be doing—and more importantly, what they themselves are doing versus what they should be doing.

While there is a place for politics in this conversation, we ought always to keep in mind that the political is merely symptomatic of our nation's spiritual condition. Our politics only reflect what we truly believe; therefore, our primary goal should not be to change people's political views. What we truly seek to change should be people's understanding of our moral responsibility before God.

The heart of a forerunner is to be on the frontlines with God's timely message wherever God calls him or her and to encourage others to do the same. Certainly, this includes fighting political causes, especially when those causes are informed by a Christian worldview. In a Democratic Republic, we have a responsibility to be aware of what is happening in our government and to seek to influence it. Our heavenly charge to serve as salt and light within the world includes the realm of politics. If we entirely disengage, then we are neglecting both our Christian duty and our obligation as citizens of this country, and we will be held culpable by God for failing to uphold righteousness and for allowing evil an opportunity to succeed at the community, state, and national levels.

As Christians, we have a responsibility to resist evil wherever we have influence, which in our country includes the national conversation. The progression of the LGBTQ+ movement is illustrative of this. Before the Supreme Court's ruling in *Obergefell v. Hodges,* many of God's people determined not to push back against homosexuality—and particularly the issue of homosexual marriages. These Christians determined to emphasize the positive elements of the Christian message rather than its warning aspects, believing that the national conversation about LGBTQ+ issues would eventually subside if we would only provide the homosexual community an opportunity to be heard. After all, the majority of Americans were, at the time, still uncomfortable with the subject of homosexuality, regardless of their religious affiliation. As such, dramatic shifts in public policy seemed unlikely. This strategy could not have proven to be more mistaken.

What Christians witnessed was an unprecedented advancement of homosexual causes in America. Activists became emboldened, intimidating politicians who increasingly felt the lack of vocal support from those who supported biblical sexuality. For all practical purposes, these activists received everything they sought, and then some. However, rather than be satisfied, like so many Christians had hoped, they chose to open a new cultural battlefront: Transgender rights.

In the beginning, these activists followed the same playbook while the church, together with most Americans, assumed the same passive posture. However, there was eventually a tipping point when the American public began pushing against proposed policies and laws. Incredibly, the response was an almost immediate relenting on the part of politicians and transgender activists.

The battle continued to rage, and still rages to this day, but those who supported transgender causes were compelled to change their tactics. More importantly, their cultural progress was substantially slowed. Often, politicians and political activists behave like young children who relentlessly push the boundaries of what is acceptable until they experience resistance. As such, there is a need for God's people to fight for righteousness in the political arena, but such battles often give rise to a dangerous mindset among God's people.

There is a temptation to view legal victories as an adequate substitution for our responsibility to change the hearts and minds of individuals. Legal victories only help to preserve an environment that is conducive to sharing the gospel and upholding God's moral standard. If we fail to take advantage of these opportunities, then legal and legislative victories are fairly meaningless because they will not change the hearts and minds of people—only their behavior. As such, we should not place a disproportionate emphasis on changing our nation's laws when our highest priority is to see hearts transformed by bringing people's thinking into alignment with the principles taught in the Bible.

CHAPTER 31

THE TASK IS A GOSPEL MISSION

It is far easier to change people's behavior than it is to change what they believe. We must resist the temptation to substitute political causes and legal victories for our responsibility to change the hearts and minds of individuals. Similarly, it can be easier to challenge the beliefs of strangers than it is to confront our family, friends, co-workers, and neighbors. Here too, we must resist the temptation to simply become anonymous keyboard warriors and faceless financial donors. It turns out making a difference is far more intimidating than we might have imagined. Meaningful and lasting difference is difficult, risky, and messy because it is personal.

Upon hearing that our nation is on a perilous trajectory that ends in divine judgment, it is natural to be moved to action in our spirits. "What can I do?" and, "How can I make a difference?" should be our instinctive response. However, these are emotional reactions that can easily prompt temporary solutions that are primarily aimed at alleviating our conscience. We may be tempted to outsource our responsibility by supporting a church, ministry, political action group, legal group, or any number of other "professionals" more qualified to make a difference. Or we might volunteer to help a particular cause.

There is value in these decisions, but they are not adequate responses to the question, "Do we want to make a difference?" The kind of difference we should seek to make is personal. When we speak of wanting to make a difference, we truly mean that we want to respond to our concern over our nation's failure to accomplish its divine mandate of drawing people back to God and the silence of God's people regarding moral matters in our culture by changing the way our friends, family, co-workers, and neighbors think about these matters. We begin making this difference by warning others of the consequences of living in continued rebellion to God's instructions, but our warning must also be followed by a call to respond in faith.

This is a grand task that will require a lifetime to complete. It is not something we can outsource to others, nor should it be a temporary phase in our lives. Instead, this is a lifelong commitment and a journey that we will only successfully complete through the empowerment of God. Fortunately, such empowerment has already been promised us. Jesus told His followers, *"I have been given all authority in heaven and on earth. Therefore, go and make disciples of all the nations, baptizing them in the name of the Father and the Son and the Holy Spirit. Teach these new disciples to obey all the commands I have given you. And be sure of this: I am with you always, even to the end of the age"* (Matt. 28:18b–20).

We are called to make new disciples and to teach them to obey God, thus our task, as forerunners, of bringing people's thinking on moral matters into conformity with God's instructions is fundamentally a gospel mission. Jesus did not confine our gospel message to a proclamation of His death, burial, and resurrection. Instead, we *apply* this proclamation. We declare the risen Jesus to be our rightful Lord who has the authority to determine how we ought to live our lives—both privately and publicly. Our warning and our call to respond in faith are both rooted in our gospel mission, and if we genuinely want to make a difference in our nation, then we must embrace Jesus' commission to become God's cultural influencers.

Part 5

BECOMING CULTURAL INFLUENCERS

CHAPTER 32

EMBRACING A DAUNTING TASK

The heart of a forerunner is burdened with discerning what is transpiring in our culture and warning others from a biblical perspective; however, the heart of a forerunner is not content merely to sound the alarm. A forerunner is also burdened with seeing the systemic change in both individuals and society that Jesus had in mind when He said, *"Go and make disciples of all the nations, baptizing them in the name of the Father and the Son and the Holy Spirit. Teach these new disciples to obey all the commands I have given you"* (Matt. 28:19–20a). Therefore, a forerunner is also necessarily a cultural influencer.

Jesus' great commission frames our Christian responsibility and is at the heart of becoming a cultural influencer, but somewhere along the line, many of us have adopted the notion that we can outsource this task to others. By financing missionaries, ministries, and the church, we assume our share of the responsibility to make disciples is complete, but this is not what Jesus had in mind. We know this because the great commission is merely a reminder of what Jesus had already taught His followers. Importantly, this previous teaching makes it clear that our responsibility cannot be outsourced to others because the focus is not on the *outcome* but the *process*.

We see this focus on the process in Matthew 5:1–14 where Jesus calls us to be *"the light of the world"* and *"the salt of the earth."* These are agents that transform the world around them because of their nature. Light illuminates—displacing darkness and exposing what otherwise could not be seen. Similarly, salt both flavors and sanitizes—it purges impurities and stops decay. Both fundamentally change that with which they come into contact. Likewise, as God's people, our interaction with the world around us ought to fundamentally change its culture as we expose spiritual lies and purge error, all with the flavor of God's love and kindness. But how do we accomplish this?

Becoming God's cultural change agents is a daunting task. Such an overwhelming responsibility can be immobilizing, or it can be invigorating. After all, who doesn't want to change the world for the better?

In order not to become paralyzed by the immensity of our assignment, it will be helpful if we consider the steps necessary to accomplish this one at a time. This will be a lengthy process. Even a cursory overview of what the Bible says about the matter will take some time, but this is a good thing. What a blessing it is that God has not assigned us such an immense task without instructions!

To help us with these instructions, God has sent us His Holy Spirit to teach and to guide us into all truth. Jesus tells His followers, *"When the Father sends the Advocate as my representative—that is, the Holy Spirit—he will teach you everything and will remind you of everything I have told you"* (John 14:26). Moreover, this is a gift that, when embraced, will produce in us *"peace of mind and heart"* (John 14:27). We need not fear this assignment, so let's begin an incredible journey of discovery as we embrace this daunting task of becoming God's cultural influencers!

CHAPTER 33

CHOOSING GOD'S SIDE

When asked whether God was on his side in the Civil War, Abraham Lincoln said, "I do not care whether God is on my side; the important question is whether I am on God's side, for God is always right."[53] It seems self-evident, but becoming God's cultural influencer begins with choosing to be on God's side regarding cultural matters.

When approaching Jericho, Joshua sees what most scholars believe to be the pre-incarnate Jesus Christ. In this passage, He is described as a man with a sword in hand. Given the fact that the Hebrews were actively invading the land of Canaan at the time, Joshua reasonably asks, *"Are you for us, or for our adversaries?"* (Josh. 5:13, ESV). The answer he receives is, *"Neither one ... I am the commander of the LORD'S army"* (Josh. 5:14). In other words, God isn't choosing sides between two armies; instead, there is God's side and everyone else's side.

If ever there was a time for God to be on Israel's side, this is it. God has personally guided the Israelites to this land, which He had promised to their forefathers. He has supernaturally dried up the Jordan River so that they could cross into this land, and He is about to miraculously collapse the walls of Jericho. Nevertheless, Jesus tells Joshua that He is not on Israel's side; neither is He on the side of Israel's enemies. Rather, He commands the army of heaven, so Joshua had best be sure to be on Jesus' side.

Earlier, God had provided a warning to Israel that serves as a principle for all nations and individuals: Choose to obey God and receive blessing, or disobey God and risk judgment (Deut. 11:26–28). These are our only choices, and there is no middle ground. Later, Jesus warns, *"Anyone who isn't with me opposes me, and anyone who isn't working with me is actually working against me"* (Matt. 12:30).

God expects us to join His side, not to invoke Him to join our side. We can choose to join God in faithful obedience to Him, or we can choose to stand in opposition to Him. Sometimes this decision can be difficult as God's side is often not where the cultural majority finds itself. Nevertheless, it is impossible to serve as God's cultural influencers if we are not in alignment with His position on cultural matters. We must choose a side.

CHAPTER 34

BREAKING THE SILENCE

A cursory assessment of America reveals that something is dreadfully wrong. We are a nation at war with God. We've embraced a self-destructive lifestyle that celebrates and flaunts the very attitudes and behaviors that incite God's judgment. Perhaps we may expect such behavior in a nation whose citizenry has openly rejected God, but 70% of Americans self-identify as "Christian."[54] As such, the silence among God's people regarding these moral issues is deafening. We should be deeply distressed over the way His people are silently tolerating rebellion to God.

As goes the church, so goes the nation. Founding father and former president John Adams writes, "Our Constitution was made only for a moral and religious People. It is wholly inadequate to the government of any other."[55] God's people serve as a moral compass guiding the course of the nation. If our nation is wayward, the responsibility rests primarily with us. Likewise, any lasting effort to correct our national course must begin with the church.

In the judgment account of Sodom and Gomorrah, we learn that God is willing to extend incredible patience and mercy to a nation in rebellion as long as there are some righteous individuals who can shine like lights in the darkness, revealing the error of people's ways and the truth of God's Word (Matt. 5:14–16; Eph. 5:8–9). Had God found as few as ten righteous individuals to contrast the rampant evil within the cities of Sodom and Gomorrah, God would have withheld His judgment (Gen. 18:22–33). Alas, not even ten righteous individuals could be found. Without righteous people to serve as a moral compass to guide these cities back to truth, all hope of national repentance was lost, leaving nothing but judgment (Gen. 19:1–17).

If God's people remain silent, refusing to expose and challenge evil, then what hope remains for our nation? Who else can guide our nation back to truth? Only God. Therefore, at some point, God Himself will be compelled to intervene with judgment designed to put an end to rebellion and wickedness.

Silence among God's people in a rebellious nation is unacceptable, and it is a precursor to divine judgment. Privately choosing to be on God's side regarding cultural matters is not enough; we need to publicly choose God's side. Becoming God's cultural influencers begins with a determination to break our silence on moral issues.

CHAPTER 35

EMBRACING OUR CALLING

It is foolish to imagine that we can be disciples of a Revolutionary without being revolutionary ourselves. As Christians, we are not called to simply keep our heads low, refusing to draw attention or distinguish ourselves from a culture that is hostile to our faith. Instead, we are to imitate Jesus, whose teaching and lifestyle was so countercultural that it captured everyone's attention—from the lowliest beggar to the most powerful leaders.

We are to serve as cultural beacons of light within our communities. Jesus tells His followers, "'*You are the light of the world—like a city on a hilltop that cannot be hidden. No one lights a lamp and then puts it under a basket. Instead, a lamp is placed on a stand, where it gives light to everyone in the house*'" (Matt. 5:14–15). As followers of Christ, we are called to reflect the unquenchable light that Jesus brought into the world (John 1:4–5).

The apostle Paul depicts this calling as an ambassadorship: "*We are Christ's ambassadors; God is making his appeal through us. We speak for Christ when we plead, 'Come back to God!'"* (2 Cor. 5:20). In other words, we are tasked with a responsibility to represent God's heart to those around us. God has strong opinions about how we live our lives, conduct our business, and govern our nation, and He has expressed these in the Bible. Therefore, God expects His ambassadors to faithfully represent His thoughts on moral issues within our culture.

When we are silent on moral matters, we fail to accurately represent Christ's heart. However, not all will appreciate being confronted by the heart of Christ. Paul warns, *"[God] uses us to spread the knowledge of Christ everywhere, like a sweet perfume. ... But this fragrance is perceived differently by those who are being saved and by those who are perishing. To those who are perishing, we are a dreadful smell of death and doom"* (2 Cor. 2:14b, 15b–16).

The smell of death is repulsive, often evoking a visceral reaction. People either flee the smell or seek to purge the source of the odor. This is the imagery Paul uses to describe our ministry because he was under no delusion that people would appreciate being confronted with the heart of Christ. He was keenly aware that such confrontation exposes the corruption of sin, often eliciting violent reactions. Nonetheless, as cultural beacons of light, God has tasked us with shining His light upon the darkness of sin in our communities. Often, this will not win the favor of those around us; nevertheless, we readily assume this responsibility *"with sincerity and with Christ's authority, knowing that God is watching us"* (2 Cor. 2:17). Therefore, becoming God's cultural influencers includes embracing our call to serve as God's representatives.

CHAPTER 36

CONTRASTING THE CULTURE

Cultural beacons of light that shine into the darkness around them necessarily contrast society (Matt. 5:14–15). Indeed, the apostle Peter takes for granted that all Christians who faithfully live according to what they profess will stand out among their family, friends, neighbors, and co-workers:

> *Even if you suffer for doing what is right, God will reward you for it. So don't worry or be afraid of their threats. Instead, you must worship Christ as Lord of your life. And if someone asks about your hope as a believer, always be ready to explain it. But do this in a gentle and respectful way. Keep your conscience clear. Then if people speak against you, they will be ashamed when they see what a good life you live because you belong to Christ* (1 Pet. 3:14–16).

We cannot effectively call people to a different lifestyle and a different hope when we ourselves are seen as living for the same things as those who are spiritually lost. Indeed, how can we say that what we believe is better than what they believe if there is no practical difference in application? If we desire to become effective change agents in our nation, then we must be willing to stand firm against worldly cultural influences (James 4:4; 1 John 2:15–17).

Unfortunately, far too many Christians have reassimilated into the very culture from which they were freed. They choose to live for the success of a sporting team; for their children's education; for their career; for a comfortable retirement; for bigger and nicer cars, houses, and furniture; for pleasure; or for any number of distractions. Moreover, they place their hope and confidence in the stock market and their retirement plans, politicians, possessions, family and relationships, their job and income, or any number of unreliable securities.

Of course, contrasting the culture does not mean we must reject everything culture has to offer. It is perfectly acceptable to listen to music, enjoy sports, drive nice vehicles, engage on social media, and enjoy other elements of our culture. However, each of these activities risks re-conforming us into the image of the world. Therefore, we must remain alert and sober minded in all that we do (1 Pet. 5:8). If we discern that anything is making us more worldly in our thinking, less godly in our actions, and more distant from the power and presence of Jesus Christ, then we should be quick to re-evaluate how we choose to engage in that activity. Likewise, we should be quick to confess when we have departed from Jesus as our first love, to repent, and to do what God has called us to do.

However we choose to engage with the world around us, we should always keep in mind that our allegiance is no longer to the things of this world. Jesus says of us, *"They do not belong to this world any more than I do"* (John 17:16). Therefore, we have no reason to measure our success by the same standards the world uses. Our success is not dependent upon our salary, the clothes we wear, the size of our house, what school our children attend, how many social media followers we've accrued, the success of our sports team, our 401(k) plan, or any other standard the world employs. Instead, our success is measured by our faithfulness to God's instructions and to our calling as ambassadors of Jesus Christ. Any lifestyle that is faithful to this mentality will necessarily differ from society. Therefore, becoming God's cultural influencers includes adopting a lifestyle whose faithfulness to God is so readily apparent that it necessarily contrasts the attitudes and behavior of our surrounding culture.

CHAPTER 37

RENEWING OUR MINDS

To contrast the culture requires that we live lives that conform to the character of Jesus rather than to cultural norms. The apostle Paul exhorts, *"Throw off your old sinful nature and your former way of life, which is corrupted by lust and deception. Instead, let the Spirit renew your thoughts and attitudes. Put on your new nature, created to be like God—truly righteous and holy"* (Eph. 4:22–24). Elsewhere he teaches, *"Don't copy the behavior and customs of this world, but let God transform you into a new person by changing the way you think. Then you will learn to know God's will for you, which is good and pleasing and perfect"* (Rom. 12:2).

God redeems His people by changing the way we think, and this is accomplished when we embrace the truth of His Word. Jesus prayed for His followers, *"Make them holy by your truth; teach them your word, which is truth. Just as you sent me into the world, I am sending them into the world. And I give myself as a holy sacrifice for them so they can be made holy by your truth"* (John 17:17–19).

Like Jesus, we should cultivate a love for the truth of God's Word. The Psalmist declares, "*Oh how I love your instructions! I think about them all day long. Your commands make me wiser than my enemies, for they are my constant guide. ... Your commandments give me understanding; no wonder I hate every false way of life. Your word is a lamp to guide my feet and a light for my path*" (Psa. 119:97–98, 104–105). Indeed, it is a commitment to the truth of God's Word that will empower us to remain righteous even as we live amongst a sinful and hostile culture. The Psalmist adds, "*I will hurry, without delay, to obey your commands. Evil people try to drag me into sin, but I am firmly anchored to your instructions*" (Psa. 119:60–61).

Our battle for righteousness begins with truth. How we think is how we will act. If we do not fight to keep our thinking firmly rooted in God's truth, we will be unable to effectively contrast the world around us, and therefore, to effect meaningful change. The apostle Peter writes, "*Prepare your minds for action and exercise self-control. ... Don't slip back into your old ways of living to satisfy your own desires. You didn't know any better then. But now you must be holy in everything you do, just as God who chose you is holy. For the Scriptures say, 'You must be holy because I am holy'*" (1 Pet. 1:13a, 14b–16).

Our culture continually bombards us with spiritual lies. If we are not intentional about immersing ourselves in the truth of God's Word, we risk embracing these lies (Psa. 119:160; 2 Cor. 10:4–5). In turn, we risk slipping into our old ways of living, which were focused on satisfying our own desires. Therefore, becoming God's cultural influencers requires a commitment to truth and a love of God's Word that continually renews our thinking.

CHAPTER 38

PROCLAIMING TRUTH

A consistent commitment to truth is difficult and costly. We should ask ourselves whether we are willing to sacrifice having a "normal" American life to fulfill our calling as Christians and to influence those around us. In other words, are we more committed to proclaiming the truth than we are to our comfort?

The apostle Peter was under no delusion that people would respect and honor Christians for standing apart from cultural deceptions. Rather, Peter expected that men would slander, accuse, and persecute God's people for being different from them and the rest of society. However, he concludes, *"Even if you suffer for doing what is right, God will reward you for it. So don't worry or be afraid of their threats. ... Remember it is better to suffer for doing good, if that is what God wants, than to suffer for doing wrong!"* (1 Pet. 3:14, 17). Similarly, Jesus encourages, *"What blessings await you when people hate you and exclude you and mock you and curse you as evil because you follow the Son of Man. When that happens, be happy! Yes, leap for joy! For a great reward awaits you in heaven"* (Luke 6:22–23a).

Jesus readily warns His followers of the difficulties that lay ahead:

> *The world would love you as one of its own if you belonged to it, but you are no longer part of the world. I chose you to come out of the world, so it hates you. Do you remember what I told you? "A slave is not greater than the master." Since they persecuted me, naturally they will persecute you. And if they had listened to me, they would listen to you* (John 15:19–20).

Regardless of what it costs us, and whether others want to hear it or choose to listen, our job is to proclaim God's truth. We give voice to God's heart, making His appeal to embrace truth (2 Cor. 5:20), but as Jesus warned, we should not expect people to respond to our appeal any differently than they responded to Him. Some respected and even accepted what Jesus said, but others were skeptical and critical (Mark 8:27–29; Luke 11:14–15). Many mocked, hated, slandered, and persecuted Him—even putting Him to death (Matt. 26:63–68; Mark 15:29–32).

The ministry of the apostle Paul illustrates what it is to follow in the footsteps of Jesus. After preaching to the intellectual elites in Athens, some mocked him, others respected him, and some believed him (Acts 17:32–34). It is not our responsibility to bring conviction—only to proclaim the truth (John 16:7–8). When we speak the truth, we flood the darkness with light, and we draw a moral line in the sand that compels people to choose sides. This is uncomfortable for both parties—we who proclaim the truth as well as those who are confronted by it (John 3:19–21; 2 Cor. 2:14–16). However, apart from truth, there can be no conviction, and apart from conviction, there can be no repentance. Therefore, becoming God's cultural influencers involves boldly proclaiming God's truth within our communities.

CHAPTER 39

WARNING OTHERS

We proclaim God's truth with a sense of urgency because the stakes are high. Likewise, we declare God's truth with boldness and with clarity because the consequences of confusion could be disastrous. And in all this, we share God's truth with a spirit of love. We cannot afford to undermine God's message by proclaiming it with an angry, judgmental, or self-righteous attitude. Instead, we *"speak the truth in love"* (Eph. 4:15).

Love does not prioritize people's feelings over truth, and it does not ignore danger, encourage irresponsible behavior, or deny reality. Rather, love warns. Love prioritizes the needs of others above our own, and it patiently endures all things as it pursues the absolute best for others (1 Cor. 13:4–7). As such, our warning, while urgent, bold, and clear, ought also to be compassionate, considerate, and genuine. The apostle Paul declares, *"My heart is filled with bitter sorrow and unending grief for my people, my Jewish brothers and sisters. I would be willing to be forever cursed—cut off from*

Christ!—if that would save them" (Rom. 9:2). Elsewhere, Paul recounts how he passionately and persistently warned the Ephesians: *"Be on your guard! Remember that for three years I never stopped warning each of you night and day with tears"* (Acts 20:31, NIV).

Paul was not alone in his compassion for those he warned. Jeremiah is remembered as the "Weeping Prophet" (Jer. 13:17). Even Jesus wept over the coming judgment upon Jerusalem, about which He had warned in Matthew chapters 23 and 24 (Luke 19:41–44).

Author and apologist Dr. Michael Brown challenges:

> When is the last time we warned someone with tears? When is the last time we cared enough to weep for them in private? May God break our hearts with the things that break His heart. May the Lord shatter our indifference. In the words of the Book of Proverbs, "Better is open rebuke than hidden love. Faithful are the wounds of a friend; profuse are the kisses of an enemy. . . . Whoever rebukes a man will afterward find more favor than he who flatters with his tongue" (Proverbs 27:5–6; 28:23). We are not called to tickle people's ears and make them feel good. We are called to speak the truth in love, to have hearts of compassion and backbones of steel, to emulate the true prophets not the false prophets, to do the right thing rather than the convenient thing.[56]

We cannot truly love others if we are unwilling to warn them of the consequences of their continued rebellion to God's instructions. Likewise, we cannot accurately represent the heart of God if we are unwilling to warn others.

Becoming God's cultural influencers requires that we fervently warn others with a boldness and clarity that stems from a place of loving compassion.

CHAPTER 40

GUARDING OUR EMOTIONS

If our battle for righteousness begins with truth, and our central calling is to both live and proclaim God's truth, then we must be continually vigilant against deception and spiritual lies. After all, our enemy is described as a deceitful schemer and a prowling lion seeking its prey: *"Put on all of God's amor so that you will be able to stand firm against all strategies of the devil. ... When [the devil] lies, it is consistent with his character; for he is a liar and the father of lies. ... Stay alert! Watch out for your great enemy, the devil. He prowls around like a roaring lion, looking for someone to devour"* (Eph. 6:11; John 8:44b; 1 Pet. 5:8).

To protect our minds and actions, we must guard our emotions. The wisest man ever to live writes, *"Guard your heart above all else, for it determines the course of your life"* (Prov. 4:23). Elsewhere, the apostle Paul cautions that anger can make us particularly susceptible to the devil's deceitful schemes: *"'Don't sin by letting anger control you.' Don't let the sun go down while you are still angry, for anger gives a foothold to the devil"* (Eph. 4:26–27).

The Greek word translated as "foothold" is *topos,* and it generally carries the idea of a place. It is also translated as a spot, a space, a room, a location, or a dwelling place.[57] In short, Paul commands us not to give the devil any opportunity to find even the smallest dwelling place in our lives. We might think of this as denying the devil the opportunity to erect a campsite within our heart, meaning the command center for our emotions.

The context speaks of becoming angry. Of all the emotions that could provide the devil a foothold, it is interesting that Paul chooses to focus on anger. Perhaps this is because we tend not to think clearly when we are angry, which makes us more susceptible to believing lies and false arguments. Thus, anger is one of the greatest threats to truth—even if that anger is justified.

What begins as a campsite for the devil can become an established dwelling place, like a home. Strong emotions, such as anger, can permit spiritual lies to penetrate our hearts, and if not quickly purged, they can become a regular part of our thinking. If we are not careful, even the smallest spiritual lie may eventually become a stronghold, establishing itself as a critical part of our worldview (2 Cor. 10:3–5). Therefore, becoming God's cultural influencers involves guarding our emotions.

CHAPTER 41

ENGAGING IDEAS

It is when we believe spiritual lies and false arguments that a demonic stronghold is established in our lives. The apostle Paul teaches, *"We are human, but we don't wage war as humans do. We use God's mighty weapons, not worldly weapons, to knock down the strongholds of human reasoning and to destroy false arguments. We destroy every proud obstacle that keeps people from knowing God. We capture their rebellious thoughts and teach them to obey Christ"* (2 Cor. 10:3–5).

Consider some of the spiritual lies embraced by our culture that have given rise to demonic strongholds:

- God just wants us to be happy (hedonism).
- There is no absolute truth (relativism).
- Our worth is defined by what we own or produce (materialism).
- God doesn't care whom we love, simply that we love (homosexuality).

- There is nothing sacred about our bodies (transgenderism).
- Sex is necessary to live a fulfilled life (pre-marital sex).
- God wouldn't want us to be trapped in a loveless marriage (divorce).
- A baby is not a real person until it is viable (abortion).
- Men and women should be equal in function (feminism).
- The well-being of this earth is more important than the well-being of humans (environmentalism).
- We have a right to decide whether we live or die (euthanasia/assisted suicide).
- The poor are poor because the rich are rich (Socialism/Communism).
- Our moral authority derives from our lived experiences (intersectionality)
- Judging some people by the color of their skin is an effective means of pushing back against a system that privileges some at the expense of others (racism).
- We must bear the guilt and shame of our ancestors (critical race theory).
- Each group should experience the same positive outcomes as every other group (social justice).

Spiritual lies are often appealing. For instance, the beloved company Disney is famous for its mantra, "Follow your heart." However, the Bible teaches, *"The human heart is the most deceitful of all things, and desperately wicked"* (Jer. 17:9a). Our hearts will lead us into error, sin, and bondage. "Follow your heart" is a spiritual lie that inevitably spawns other lies, such as, "It's all about you;" "Just be yourself;" "Speak your truth;" "Love conquers all;" "I'm gay and that's OK;" "If it feels good do it;" and so many more.

If we hope to influence our culture, then we must engage ideas. These ideas may manifest themselves in the form of political causes, lifestyle choices, attitudes, addictions, etc., but at their core is a spiritual lie. Therefore, becoming God's cultural influencers involves engaging ideas by countering spiritual lies with the truth of God's Word.

CHAPTER 42

BECOMING INFORMED

Before we can effectively engage cultural ideas and the spiritual lies that undergird them, we must be informed. God wants His people to be knowledgeable: *"Intelligent people are always ready to learn. Their ears are open for knowledge"* (Prov. 18:15). Indeed, it is difficult both to identify and to counter spiritual lies when we are uninformed.

Becoming informed begins with being aware of what is happening in our communities. However, awareness is only the first step. Knowing about something is not the same as understanding the matter. Likewise, knowing what we "should" believe about something is not the same as being informed.

Far too many people are happy to outsource their critical thinking to a particular news source, the host of a talk radio show or a podcast, a trusted friend, social media polls, memes, or a political party. However, Proverbs warns, *"Only simpletons believe everything they're told! The prudent carefully consider their steps. ... Simpletons are clothed with foolishness, but the prudent are crowned with knowledge"* (Prov. 14:15, 18).

Granted, we live in an information age where it is easy to become overwhelmed by the quantity of information vying for our attention. It is far more convenient to simply memorize talking points than it is to sort through the noise and to piece together the relevant details necessary to critically evaluate the matter. Nonetheless, God expects His change agents to be knowledgeable about the cultural lies we are confronting. This does not require that we be highly educated on everything transpiring around us, but it does mean that we should have a robust understanding of the issues we choose to confront. Proverbs warns, *"Spouting off before listening to the facts is both shameful and foolish"* (Prov. 18:13).

True understanding of cultural issues will necessarily involve news networks, social media, talk radio, and podcasts, but while these may serve to supply us with facts, they should not be our wellsprings for determining what we ought to think and for judging between right and wrong. While such resources are helpful in providing facts and educated opinions, they are often devoid of a biblical foundation and worldview. God's people should view all things firstly through a biblical lens—not a partisan political perspective or according to a cultural narrative. We should be able to engage ideas from a familiarity with the Bible and God's heart, not just a familiarity with political talking points and cultural norms. After all, the *"fear of the LORD is the foundation of true knowledge"* (Prov. 1:7a).

As we pursue understanding, our prayer ought always to be, *"I believe in your commandments; now teach me good judgment and knowledge ... Show me the right path, O LORD; point out the road for me to follow"* (Psa. 119:66; 25:4). Becoming God's cultural influencers necessitates becoming informed—not only of the facts, but also of God's heart on political and social matters.

CHAPTER 43

DISCOVERING RELIABLE RESOURCES

A willingness and desire to become informed is only the first step. The next is to discover useful resources that can help us become educated on cultural issues from a biblical perspective. Keeping in mind that every ministry has room for improvement and areas where we may differ, below are some recommended starting points.

- Albert Mohler – President of Southern Theological Seminary Dr. Albert Mohler provides a blog and two podcasts. Particularly notable is The Briefing podcast, which is a 20-minute daily analysis of news and current events from a Christian worldview.
  - **www.AlbertMohler.com**

- Alisa Childers – Former member of the band Zoe Girl, Alisa Childers has a heart for addressing progressive Christianity. Her blog and podcast focus on apologetics, theology, culture, and worship.
  - **www. AlisaChilders.com**

- Allie Beth Stuckey – Author of *Your Not Enough (& That's Okay): Escaping the Toxic Culture of Self-Love*, Allie's Relatable podcast tackles the most pressing issues facing our country and the Christian church, from national politics and the culture wars to theology, by analyzing culture, news, and politics from a biblically reformed and politically conservative perspective.
  - **www.AllieBethStuckey.com**

- AskDrBrown Ministries – The author of more than 40 books and numerous articles, Dr. Michael Brown is the founder and president of FIRE School of Ministry and the host of the Line of Fire, a daily, nationally syndicated talk radio show. He is widely considered to be the world's foremost Messianic Jewish apologist and is a national and international speaker on the themes of spiritual renewal and cultural reformation.
  - **www.AskDrBrown.org**

- Bible Project – Focused on helping people experience the Bible as a unified story that leads to

Jesus, the Bible Project produces short cartoon videos and a podcast that expresses deep truths in a simple and conversational manner.

- **www.BibleProject.com**

- Bible Thinker – This is a ministry of Mike Winger that is dedicated to equipping people to think and live biblically. His confidence is in the sufficiency and truth of the Bible and the Christian worldview to not only inform us of the reality and truth of Jesus and the Bible, but to equip us to live all of life rightly and to worship God in truth.

    - **www.BibleThinker.org**

- Capitol Hill Baptist Church – Located in our nation's political hub, this evangelical church offers sermons, seminars, and articles that apply the Bible to cultural and political issues.

    - **www.CapitolHillBaptist.org**

- Epoch Times – Striving to provide a truthful view of the world free from the influence of any government, corporation, or political party, this newspaper belongs to the category of independent news media. It aims to report what it sees, not how to think. Although this newspaper is not Christian, it does promote traditional values.

    - **www.TheEpochTimes.com**

- Forerunners of America – This ministry is focused on warning about the national consequences of ignoring God's moral commands and helping Christians respond in faith so that they can stand firm and minister through times of increasing difficulty. Forerunners of America provides timely messages on cultural issues through podcasts, articles, Bible study materials, books, apologetic resources, and conferences.
  - **www.ForerunnersOfAmerica.org**

- Good Fight Ministries – Pastor Joe Schimmel produces sermons, documentaries, podcasts, and articles on the topics of music, Hollywood, cults, the occult, pop culture, and prophecy to help Christians understand the times in which we are living from a Christian perspective.
  - **www.GoodFight.org**

- Got Questions – This is an online database of evangelical answers to commonly asked questions. To date, Got Questions has endeavored to answer approximately 700,000 Bible questions.
  - **www.GotQuestions.org**

- Koinonia House – This ministry of the late Chuck Missler exists to create, develop, and distribute materials to stimulate, encourage, and facilitate serious study of the Bible as the inerrant Word of

God. Koinonia House provides a radio broadcast, podcast, blog, weekly news updates, a monthly news journal, and seminary-level verse-by-verse book studies for the entire Bible, as well as numerous topical studies.

- **www.KHouse.org**

- Michael Heiser – Dr. Michael Heiser is an author, an academic scholar, a professor of theology and biblical studies, a former scholar-in-residence for Logos Bible Software, and founder of MEMRA and Awakening School of Theology and Ministry. He hosts several blogs and podcasts ranging from refuting ancient aliens and exploring popular topics in fringe history to exegetical Bible study. His blogs and podcasts are designed to minister to those who seek to understand the Bible in its original and supernatural context.

  - **www.DrMSH.com**

- One Minute Apologist – Bobby Conway provides brief and credible answers to apologetic questions that resource people with a hunger to defend their Christian faith.

  - **www.OneMinuteApologist.com**

- Remnant Radio – Endeavoring to educate Christians in biblical theology and a Christian worldview without boring anyone to sleep, Joshua Lewis,

Michael Rowntree, and Michael Miller provide a conversational podcast that explores the many theological perspectives within Christendom with an open mind that seeks to root everything in Scripture.

- **www.RemnantRadio.com**

CHAPTER 44

PREPARING FOR BATTLE

"Be strong in the Lord and in his mighty power. Put on all of God's armor so that you will be able to stand firm against all strategies of the devil. ... and take up the sword of the Spirit, which is the word of God" (Eph. 6:10–11, 17b). God has equipped us with a unique weapon for confronting the spiritual lies that have produced demonic strongholds within our culture.

No talking point, presentation of facts, logical argument, or emotional appeal can compare to the effectiveness of this supernatural weapon. This is why the apostle Paul writes, *"We use God's mighty weapons, not worldly weapons, to knock down the strongholds of human reasoning and to destroy false arguments"* (2 Cor. 10:4).

Error simply cannot prevail against the truth of God's Word, which *"corrects us when we are wrong and teaches us to do what is right"* (2 Tim. 3:16b). Why then would we ever consider engaging cultural ideas without first equipping ourselves with the Bible? There simply is no better resource for understanding the heart and mind of God on any matter than the Bible because it is the very Word of God (2 Tim. 3:16; 2 Pet. 1:20–21).

With the Bible, we possess the words that created matter from nothing (Gen. 1:1–27). We possess the words that broke the authority of Satan and death in our lives (John 19:30). We possess the words that struck instant fear into the hearts of a myriad of demons (Luke 8:27–32). We possess the words that declared the end from the beginning (Isa. 46:9–10). And we possess the words that will ultimately conquer all who oppose God (Rev. 19:15).

In our battle against cultural ideas, the Bible is indispensable because only it is powerful enough to discern and counter even the most cunning and complicated spiritual lie: *"The Word of God is alive and powerful. It is sharper than the sharpest two-edged sword, cutting between soul and spirit, between joint and marrow. It exposes our innermost thoughts and desires"* (Heb. 4:12). Therefore, becoming God's cultural influencers necessitates equipping ourselves with God's Word.

CHAPTER 45

WIELDING GOD'S TRUTH

"We are human, but we don't wage war as humans do. We use God's mighty weapons, not worldly weapons, to knock down the strongholds of human reasoning and to destroy false arguments" (2 Cor. 10:3–4). Chief among these otherworldly weapons is the Bible. The apostle Paul exhorts us, *"Take the sword of the Spirit, which is the word of God"* (Eph. 6:17b).

Despite being described as a double-edged sword of the finest craftsmanship (Heb. 4:12), our appreciation for the power of this weapon is diminished because even the best of swords is no match for today's modern arsenal of guns, missiles, and smart bombs. Nevertheless, at the time that Paul was writing, there was a special kind of sword that was the superweapon of its day. When Paul says the Bible can be likened to a sword, he used the term *machaira*, which is the title for this particular superweapon.

Being uneducated in swordplay, if we were to choose a sword with which to do battle, most of us would likely gravitate toward a large broadsword. After all, our American mentality often assumes that bigger equals better, so we might choose a massive sword like the Scottish Claymore. The Greeks had a word for such swords. It is *rhomphaia*, and it refers to a sword that is at least a meter long.[58] However, through the inspiration of the Holy Spirit, Paul refers to the Bible as a *machaira*, which is a kind of sword so short that it might be mistaken for a dagger.[59] Of course, this begs the question, "How could such a short sword be the superweapon of its day?"

Greek soldiers practiced extensively to master the skill of using the short sword because the *machaira* requires great skill and precision to deliver a fatal blow. However, once mastered, the *machaira* gave the Greek soldiers a quickness and agility that could not be countered. Soldiers using the heavy broadsword simply could not parry fast enough to counter the Greek short sword. This new weapon revolutionized warfare in the ancient world and contributed to the rise of the Greek empire. Even in Paul's day, it was a highly feared and respected weapon.

The *machaira* is an apt analogy for the Bible. Just as the *machaira* was only deadly in the hand of a master swordsman who spent considerable time familiarizing himself with his weapon, so also the Bible only becomes a superweapon in the hands of a Christian who has spent considerable time studying and familiarizing himself with the text. Moreover, Paul refers to the Bible as the *rhema* of God rather than *logos*. In his *Complete Word Study Dictionary*, Spiros Zodhiates notes that *logos* generally conveys "the expression of thought, while rhema stands for the subject matter of the word or the thing which is spoken about."[60] Specifically, *rhema* is a spoken statement, and the "*rhema* of God," according to Zodhiates, is based on "the doctrines and promises of God revealed and taught in the Bible."[61] Thus, when Paul exhorts us to take up the sword of the Spirit, he calls it the statement/doctrines/promises of God, which only furthers Paul's imagery of the Bible as a *machaira*—a precise weapon requiring great skill in handling.

We do not break the skulls of demons by broadly swinging our Bible. Spiritual warfare is not fought using broad and general statements. Rather, spiritual warfare is precise. Specific verses of Scripture espousing God's promises and doctrines are used to defend and attack against different spiritual lies. God expects His people to be so familiar with His Word that we can readily call forth the exact statement needed to counter the spiritual lie at hand. Our lives are to be so saturated with the Word of God that we know exactly where to turn when facing any struggle or temptation. Indeed, this is precisely the example that Jesus set forth when He was enticed by Satan. Jesus did not battle Satan's temptation by saying generally, "No, because the Bible says so." Instead, He used specific verses of Scripture to refute the devil's schemes (Luke 4:1–13).

Thankfully, we are promised help in this endeavor. If we will commit to studying and applying God's Word to our lives, then the Holy Spirit will help bring these specific statements/doctrines/promises of God to remembrance when we need them (Matt. 10:19). Jesus pledged, "*When the*

Father sends the Advocate as my representative—that is, the Holy Spirit—he will teach you everything and will remind you of everything I have told you" (John 14:26). Therefore, becoming God's cultural influencers requires so familiarizing ourselves with God's truth that we are capable of precisely applying it to spiritual lies.

CHAPTER 46

BECOMING VOCAL

More is necessary for us to engage cultural ideas and the spiritual lies that undergird them than simply becoming informed and equipped with God's Word. We must also *wield* God's truth, and this means becoming vocal. It matters little how informed we are if we do nothing with that information.

Keep in mind that our primary goal should not be to change a person's political views. Rather, we combat spiritual lies with the truth of God's Word in order to provoke conviction of heart and repentance. For fellow Christians, this strengthens their faith and their relationship with God. For those who are not yet believers, our goal is to see the transforming power of the gospel free them from the bondage of sin and the power of the devil.

In today's age, becoming vocal can involve a variety of platforms.

- **Home** – We may have no greater platform than our kitchen table. Are we capitalizing on this platform? Are we building relationships and creating opportunities to share the truth by inviting people into our homes for games, a movie, dinner, or desert? Are we using our homes to host a prayer gathering for our community and nation, a small group Bible study to help people stand firm in their faith, or a discussion group regarding what we are observing in our culture?

- **Relationships** – Are we intentional about seizing opportunities to share the truth in our relationships? Are we bold enough to speak God's truth into the lives of our family and friends? What about those with whom we don't yet have an established relationship but with whom we regularly interact at our children's school, the store, the gym, work, or church?

- **Church** – Are we seeking opportunities to teach a class or a small group study in our church? Are those of us who choose not to teach, but who participate in such groups, regularly sharing our perspective with the class? What about our conversations in the hallways and fellowship areas of church? Are we intentional in how we approach these discussions?

- **Work** – Are we intentional when we speak with our co-workers about their life experiences? Do we challenge workplace policies that undermine truth?

- **Internet** – Are we using social media to influence people's thinking? For what posts do we choose to like, share, and comment? Do we engage in forums? Do we have a blog, a podcast, or a video channel where we can speak the truth?

- **Mailbox** – Are we mailing ministry newsletters, written letters, or cards that inform, exhort, and encourage people in truth? What about our digital mailboxes? Are we utilizing e-mail effectively?

- **Phone** – We may have no more convenient platform than the telephone. Are we intentional about connecting with people via our phones? Do we use our phone calls and text messages to promote God's truth? Are we purposefully staying connected with people in conversation so as to be able to speak into their lives regarding relevant issues?

Becoming God's cultural influencers involves finding our voice. Never have God's people been blessed with so many opportunities to be vocal. Whether we choose to speak face-to-face or via a medium such as the internet or telephone, we need to give voice to God's truth within our communities.

CHAPTER 47

BECOMING OFFENSIVE

Informed and vocal change agents who confront spiritual lies by engaging cultural ideas with the truth of God's Word will cause offense. This is because truth compels people to face the ugly reality of their actions, along with their consequences. This is why the apostle Paul writes, *"To those who are perishing, we are a dreadful smell of death and doom"* (2 Cor. 2:16a).

Many will flee the truth, and others will seek to silence it. Nevertheless, some will be so repulsed by their behavior that they will repent and embrace God's offer of deliverance. Therefore, Paul adds, *"But to those who are being saved, we are a life-giving perfume"* (2 Cor. 2:16b).

God's people cannot be afraid of offending others with His truth because freedom from the corrupting influence of sin only comes through a committed understanding of truth (John 8:31–32). Indeed, we have an obligation to speak God's truth, even if it causes offense: *"Speaking the truth in love, we are to grow up in every way into him who is the head, into*

Christ" (Eph. 4:15, ESV). Note, however, that there is an expectation that we will do this in the most tender, yet meaningful, way possible.

People do not change unless they are first offended by their own behavior. In this sense, the truth should, and must, offend. But this offense ought to stem from the conviction of the Holy Spirit, not from the force of our delivery: *"[The Holy Spirit] will convict the world of its sin, and of God's righteousness, and of the coming judgment"* (John 16:8).

If we are overly concerned about causing discomfort or offense, then we will likely never see meaningful change. Even Jesus was not more concerned about people's feelings than their need to embrace truth. Jesus regularly reached out to those whom society rejected as sinful reprobates, but He did not build relationships with sinners just to make them feel loved. Instead, He wanted to see them freed from their sin. After first demonstrating His genuine concern for their wellbeing, Jesus was not afraid to offend sinners with the truth because Jesus never placed people's feelings above their need for salvation.

This is the tough love to which we are called: *"I am giving you a new commandment: Love each other. Just as I have loved you, you should love each other"* (John 13:34). Becoming God's cultural influencers includes showing a tough love that is honest enough to elicit offense for the purpose of conviction.

CHAPTER 48

LOVING OTHERS

Great confusion surrounds the nature of love in our society. At the risk of oversimplifying, we've equated love with a feeling of being special. Indeed, much of the infatuation we today call love is merely a sophisticated form of selfishness. We feel special when we are with somebody, and as such, we treat that person as special, thus making the person feel loved. This is basically the plot of most romantic movies; however, this view of love is far less innocent than it appears on film.

Our society has elevated this distorted concept of love as the ultimate virtue. As such, making someone feel unloved has become one of our culture's greatest crimes. Given that love is equated with a feeling of being special, this crime centers around anything that makes a person feel unappreciated, misunderstood, rejected, or uncomfortable. Therefore, causing offense by exposing personal beliefs, lifestyle choices, and behaviors as spiritual lies is touted as being unloving—a nearly unforgivable crime worthy of being "cancelled" in our culture.

If this is true, then Jesus was far from a loving individual because He was constantly speaking offensive truths. Consider what He told the Pharisees: *"You are like whitewashed tombs—beautiful on the outside but filled on the inside with dead people's bones and all sorts of impurity. Outwardly you look like righteous people, but inwardly your hearts are filled with hypocrisy and lawlessness. ... Snakes! Sons of vipers! How will you escape the judgment of hell?"* (Matt. 23:27b–28, 33).

In reality, biblical love is far less concerned about our feelings than it is about truth. Jesus tells Nicodemus that God loves the whole world enough to sacrifice His only son so that anyone can be restored in His relationship with God (John 3:16–17), but He also says, *"Anyone who does not believe in him has already been judged for not believing in God's one and only Son"* (John 3:18). God's love, alone, is not sufficient to procure our salvation because true love refuses to overlook sin. To be saved, we need to identify our sin, turn from it, and submit our will to Jesus: *"If you openly declare that Jesus is Lord and believe in your heart that God raised him from the dead, you will be saved. For it is by believing in your heart that you are made right with God, and it is by openly declaring your faith that you are saved"* (Rom. 10:9–10).

True love calls people to repentance because it is what they truly need. It refuses to prioritize feelings and to turn a blind eye to wickedness. Instead, it speaks God's truth about our thinking and behavior. We should not be needlessly offensive, but we must love others enough to speak truth to error, even when it hurts. Becoming God's cultural influencers requires a commitment to biblical love and to Jesus' example of loving others by speaking truth into their lives.

CHAPTER 49

EMBRACING DIFFICULTY

The fear of experiencing difficulty can be paralyzing. Nevertheless, it is often during times of trial and tribulation that the gospel is best spread. At times, God may utilize seasons of difficulty to redirect His people toward new assignments.

The testimony of Philip illustrates this point and provides insight into a mindset that embraces difficulty. When fleeing *"a great wave of persecution,"* shortly after Jesus' ascension to heaven, Philip seized upon the opportunity to preach the gospel in new areas (Acts 8:1–5). He could have become bitter over being compelled to leave his home and country because of his commitment to God. Instead, he preached Christ, and many people were saved.

What motivated Philip to preach rather than become bitter? Of this we can only speculate:

- He had a proper perspective. He understood that the trials of this life are temporary and fleeting in comparison to our future glory (Rom. 8:18; 2 Cor. 4:16–18).

- He trusted in the sovereignty of God who created all things and reigns as King of kings and Lord of lords (Acts 4:24; 1 Tim. 6:15).
- He had already weighed the cost of following Jesus. Philip served a Lord who had sacrificed everything for him and who had called him to be willing to sacrifice everything in return (Matt. 10:37–39).
- He cared about people. This is likely the same Philip who served as a deacon, caring for the neglected widows in Jerusalem (Acts 6:1–7). Moreover, his choice to minister to the Samaritans reveals his concern for people because the Jews despised the Samaritans, but Philip refused to overlook them.
- He followed the leading of the Holy Spirit and relied upon the power of God in his ministry (Acts 8:29–30).

Rather than shun difficulty, let us embrace it, trusting in the sovereignty of God: "*We know that God causes everything to work together for the good of those who love God and are called according to his purpose for them*" (Rom. 8:28). Indeed, when times of adversity come, we are often confronted with problems and pressures that are too big for us to resolve in our own strength. In those moments, God is revealed as our provider, our strength, and our shield during times of difficulty (Psa. 18:1–3; 2 Cor. 12:7–10). And when these qualities of God are on full display in our lives, they become powerful tools of evangelism.

When our attitudes and actions are righteous, despite our circumstances, we shine like lights, contrasting the darkness of the world around us (Php. 2:14–15). People are drawn to our hope when we are not afraid or discouraged by our circumstances, and this provides meaningful opportunities to share the gospel (1 Pet. 3:14–15). Therefore, becoming God's cultural influencers includes adopting a mindset that embraces difficulty because we trust in the sovereignty of God.

CHAPTER 50

VALUING ADVERSITY

As children of God, we need not fear experiencing times of difficulty. This is true even if God should choose to judge our nation for its waywardness. While nobody wants to experience difficulties, it is often during times of trial and tribulation that the gospel is best spread (Acts 8:1–4). Moreover, God uses adversity to focus, to redirect, and to strengthen His people. This is why James encourages us, *"When troubles of any kind come your way, consider it an opportunity for great joy. For you know that when your faith is tested, your endurance has a chance to grow"* (James 1:2b–3).

Pressure is a necessary component of conforming, and we are being conformed into the image of Jesus Christ (Rom. 8:29, ESV). The pressure of difficulty aids in molding our character and attitudes into the likeness of Jesus. This is why the apostle Paul can say, *"We can rejoice, too, when we run into problems and trials, for we know that they help us develop endurance. And endurance develops strength of character, and character strengthens our confident hope of salvation"* (Rom. 5:3–5).

Sometimes this process of conformity involves purging sin, and, at other times, it involves strengthening character and resolve. According to the Institute for Basic Life Principles, God uses adversity to:

- Expose pride (Prov. 11:2; 29:23)
- Motivate us to cry out to God (Psa. 34:17; 2 Chron. 7:13–14)
- Purify our faith and develop patience (James 1:3; 1 Pet. 1:6–7)
- Strengthen our hatred for sin because when we experience the damaging effects of sin, our hatred for evil increases (Gal. 6:7–8)
- Cause us to desire more of Jesus Christ's power in our lives because troubles reveal that, in our own strength, we are unable to consistently live in a way that honors God (Php. 3:8–10)

Moreover, adversity encourages repentance when necessary. It reminds us that God is always present and that we are accountable to Him for our every thought, word, and deed. The Bible reveals that fear of the Lord is the key to life, wisdom, and lasting achievement (Prov. 9:10; 14:27; 22:4). If we lose our awareness of God and begin to think and act as if He does not exist, He may allow painful reminders of our need for Him. It is better if we experience the temporary discomfort of God's corrective discipline than suffer the destruction that inevitably results from setting our will and desires against those of God (Heb. 12:5–11).

Regardless of our circumstances, *"We know that God causes everything to work together for the good of those who love God and are called according to his purpose for them"* (Rom. 8:28). Becoming God's cultural influencers involves internalizing this truth so that we can value adversity, embracing difficulty with joyful hearts.

CHAPTER 51

DRAWING NEAR TO GOD'S HEART

In times of adversity, we are encouraged to draw near to God: *"Let us then with confidence draw near to the throne of grace, that we may receive mercy and find grace to help in time of need"* (Heb. 4:16, ESV). This is precisely what Jesus did throughout His earthly ministry. When facing adversity, Jesus chose to focus upon God's heart rather than His personal desires.

Jesus was tempted in all the same ways as us, yet He was without sin (Heb. 4:15). Given that James teaches, *"Temptation comes from our own desires, which entice us and drag us away"* (James 1:14), we must conclude that Jesus experienced a full range of emotional responses to adversity, just as we do. The difference being that Jesus refused to succumb to those desires that would have produced sin (James 1:15). Instead, Jesus drew near to God, so as to learn His Father's heart. In other words, Jesus chose to prioritize the desires of His Father above His own, and He acted accordingly (John 5:30; 12:49).

Jesus' solution for holiness may sound simple, but it came with great suffering (Heb. 2:18). We can only imagine how intense His personal struggle may have been. After all, the author of Hebrews reminds us that none of us have ever endured temptation to the point of death, the way Jesus did (Heb. 12:4). Indeed, Jesus' temptation provoked loud cries of pleading and tears (Heb. 5:7–8). So great was His stress and agony that His sweat became great drops of blood (Luke 22:43) Nonetheless, even in this greatest moment of trial, Jesus chose to draw near to His Father, praying, "'*Father, if you are willing, please take this cup of suffering away from me. Yet I want your will to be done, not mine*'" (Luke 22:42).

Jesus modelled for us how to effectively overcome our sinful desires. We do this by relinquishing them to God and by embracing God's heart on every matter. Therefore, let us take full advantage of our access to God and draw near to Him in boldness so that we can learn His heart (Heb. 4:16). Then we will be able to accurately represent God in all things and in all circumstances. Becoming God's cultural influencers requires that we draw near to God, prayerfully seeking His heart on every matter.

CHAPTER 52

COMMUNICATING WITH GOD

The apostle Paul exhorts us, *"Never stop praying"* (1 Thess. 5:17). Elsewhere, he writes, *"Don't worry about anything; instead, pray about everything. Tell God what you need, and thank him for all he has done. Then you will experience God's peace, which exceeds anything we can understand"* (Php. 4:6–7a). Prayer reorients our perspective and invites God into our life circumstances.

Prayer was an important part of Jesus' ministry, although we are given only a few details (Luke 5:16). Nevertheless, we can surmise the nature of His prayers by the way He taught His disciples to pray (Matt. 6:9–13). Every point in the Lord's prayer is designed to draw the supplicant near to God by internalizing the core teachings of Jesus, who spoke only what He received from His Father (John 8:26).

- **Our Father in heaven** – Understand that God's heart toward us is that of a father. God is not the harsh and disconnected caricature that society has imagined. Instead, He is loving, gracious, merciful, and patient toward us, His children, and He desires only what is absolutely best for us.

- **May your name be kept holy** – As those who are baptized into the name of God and called to serve as His representatives, we sully the name of God when we choose to live in unrepentant sin (Matt. 28:19; 2 Cor. 5:20). How can we boldly approach the throne of a holy God if we are not willing to relent of our sinful behavior (Heb. 4:16)? Because God loves us, He will not ignore unrepentant sin. Instead, as with any loving father, He will discipline us (Heb. 12:5–11).

- **May your kingdom come soon** – There is a clash of kingdoms occurring as heaven invades earth (Luke 11:20–22). Being citizens of heaven, our desire should be to see God's kingdom expand (Php. 3:20). We cannot permit our hearts to reassimilate into the kingdom of darkness from which we have been delivered (Col. 1:13–14; Rev. 18:2–4).

- **May your will be done on earth, as it is in heaven** – We must be willing to prioritize God's desires over our own. We are called to represent God's heart (2 Cor. 5:20). This involves embracing a new way of thinking. As faithful ambassadors, we offer ourselves as living sacrifices, wholly devoted to seeing God's will fulfilled on earth (Rom. 12:1–2).

- **Give us today the food we need** – Just as God supernaturally provided for the needs of the Israelites in the wilderness, so also, we trust God to provide for our daily needs (Exo. 16:12–18, 35). In doing so, we hold tightly to nothing, recognizing that our belongings are a gift from God (Ecc. 5:19; Acts 4:32–35; 2 Cor. 9:6–10) and that we serve as stewards of God's blessings (1 Pet. 4:9–10).

- **Forgive us our sins** – We have been washed of our sins by the blood of Jesus and the Word of God (Eph. 5:25–26; 1 John 1:7). Nonetheless, we may still get our spiritual feet dirty (John 13:10). In such moments, we should be quick to seek cleansing (1 John 1:8–9).

- **As we have forgiven those who sin against us** – We pay forward the loving forgiveness of Jesus we have received. Anything less would be a failure to accurately represent the heart of God (Col. 3:12–13). Without limit, we readily relinquish our right to seek recompense or retribution (Matt. 18:21–22).

- **Don't let us yield to temptation** – In His mercy, God refuses to permit greater temptation than we can bear (1 Cor. 10:13). God provides not only a way of escape but also the aid of His Holy Spirit, who helps us to recall the teachings of Jesus (John 14:26).

- **Rescue us from the evil one** – God has already redeemed us from the curse of the law and delivered us from the kingdom of darkness (Gal. 1:3–4; 3:13; Col. 1:13–14). Now, all we need do is submit ourselves to God and resist the devil, and he will flee from us (James 4:7). God surrounds the godly with protection and with shouts of deliverance (Psa. 32:6–7; Prov. 18:10).

So much truth is packed into such a short and simple prayer! The effectiveness of our prayer life should not be determined by the length of time we spend praying but by the degree to which we align our thinking with the character and will of God (Matt. 6:7). If we continually pray in this way, then we can rejoice in any and every circumstance as we boldly proclaim God's truth (1 Thess. 5:16–18). Therefore, becoming God's cultural influencers includes communicating with God in a manner that internalizes God's truth and effectively re-orients our thinking around God's will for our lives and nation.

CHAPTER 53

PARTICIPATING WITH GOD THROUGH PRAYER

James exhorts us to *"draw near to God"* (James 4:8, ESV). Likewise, the Psalmist encourages us to *"seek his presence continually"* (Psa. 105:4, ESV). One means of accomplishing this is through prayer.

There are many ways we can foster a meaningful prayer life:

- Abide in the instructions of Jesus (John 15:7).
- Devote a consistent time to concentrated prayer (Psa. 5:3; Luke 18:1–8).
- Maintain an attitude that continually invites God into our activities and seeks His counsel (1 Thess. 5:17).
- Be thankful and express our gratitude to God (Php. 4:6).

- Believe that God is listening to our prayers (Psa. 34:15; 1 John 5:14).
- Believe that God desires to respond to our prayers (Matt. 21:22).
- Understand that, while God is not obligated to respond to our prayers, He is a merciful God who does hear and respond (Dan. 9:18).
- Understand that unconfessed sin interferes with our prayers (Psa. 66:18; James 5:16).
- Ask for things that align themselves with the heart of God rather than our personal desires (James 4:3).
- Ask things of God boldly and with confidence (Heb. 4:16).
- Submit our will and understanding to God, knowing that He knows best (Mark 9:24).

Not only does prayer move our hearts closer to God but it can also move God's heart. James writes, *"The earnest prayer of a righteous person has great power and produces wonderful results"* (James 5:16b). In other words, God responds to our prayers. Indeed, when Moses pleaded with God for mercy upon the Hebrews (Exo. 32:11–13), the Bible records, *"The LORD changed his mind about the terrible disaster he had threatened to bring on his people"* (Exo. 32:14). Incredibly, this happened not once but twice (Num. 14:17–20)!

Philosopher Blaise Pascal writes, "God has instituted prayer so as to confer upon His creatures the dignity of being causes."[62] Similarly, author and pastor John Mark Comer writes:

> Prayer is what Moses did with God in the tent. What Jesus did with the Father in Gethsemane. It's brutally honest, naked, and vulnerable. It's when your deepest desires and fears and hopes and dreams leak out of your mouth with no inhibition. It's when you talk to God with the edit button in the *off* position and you feel safe and heard and loved. It's the kind of relational exchange you can't get enough of. And our prayers make a difference. … Our prayers have the potential to alter the course of history. And God's action *in* history is, in some strange way, contingent on our prayers.[63]

In other words, prayer is when we express to God how we feel about our experiences and the world around us, and it is when we share our feelings and ideas for how God's will may best be accomplished. Skye Jethani writes:

> We are not merely passive set pieces in a prearranged cosmic drama, but we are active participants with God in the writing, directing, design, and action that unfolds. Prayer, therefore, is much more than asking God for this or that outcome. It is drawing into communion with him and there taking up our privileged role as his people. In prayer, we are invited to join him in directing the course of his world.[64]

Therefore, one of the most effective ways of becoming God's cultural influencers is to participate with God in prayer.

CHAPTER 54

DRAWING NEAR TO GOD IN OUR DESIRES

A well-known tale, commonly misattributed to Native Americans,[65] was first published by famed evangelist Billy Graham in his book, *The Holy Spirit: Activating God's Power in Your Life*:

> An Eskimo fisherman came to town every Saturday afternoon. He always brought his two dogs with him. One was white and the other was black. He had taught them to fight on command. Every Saturday afternoon in the town square the people would gather and these two dogs would fight and the fisherman would take bets. On one Saturday the black dog would win; another Saturday, the white dog would win—but the fisherman always won! His friends began to ask him how he did it. He said, "I starve one and feed the other. The one I feed always wins because he is stronger."[66]

Applying this parable to our spiritual lives, Graham concludes, "We have two natures within us, both struggling for mastery. Which one will dominate us? It depends on which one we feed. If we feed our spiritual lives and allow the Holy Spirit to empower us, He will have rule over us. If we starve our spiritual natures and instead feed the old, sinful nature, the flesh will dominate."[67]

This internal conflict is the same principle taught by the apostle Paul:

> *So I say, let the Holy Spirit guide your lives. Then you won't be doing what your sinful nature craves. The sinful nature wants to do evil, which is just the opposite of what the Spirit wants. And the Spirit gives us desires that are the opposite of what the sinful nature desires. These two forces are constantly fighting each other, so you are not free to carry out your good intentions* (Gal. 5:16–17).

The cravings of our sinful nature include sexual immorality, impurity, sensuality, idolatry, sorcery, enmity, strife, jealousy, fits of anger, rivalries, dissensions, divisions, envy, drunkenness, orgies, and similar behavior (Gal. 5:19–21). In contrast, the Holy Spirit produces love, joy, peace, patience, kindness, goodness, faithfulness, gentleness, and self-control (Gal. 5:22–23). When we fix our minds upon these things, we feed the white dog within us (Php. 4:8). Likewise, when we refuse to participate in the behavior and lusts of the world, we starve the black dog (Rom. 8:2; 1 John 2:15–17).

Becoming God's cultural influencers involves drawing near to God in our desires. In doing this, we will become increasingly renewed in our thinking and "*will learn to know God's will*" (Rom. 12:2). Indeed, when our desires are aligned with God's desires, nothing will prove to be impossible (Job 42:2; Luke 1:37; Php. 4:13).

CHAPTER 55

TUNING IN TO THE HOLY SPIRIT

Before the digital era, it was common for radios to simultaneously receive signals from two separate stations—particularly while driving. Generally, neither station was especially clear as each vied for dominance. When this happened, the radio dial would need to be slightly adjusted to retune to the preferred station. Once this adjustment was made and the signal was strong again, the other station could no longer be heard. The signal from the suppressed station was still being transmitted across the airwaves, but the strength of the other signal, combined with the fine tuning of the radio, prevented it from being heard. This is a superb analogy of our spiritual struggle.

The apostle Paul teaches:

Let the Holy Spirit guide your lives. Then you won't be doing what your sinful nature craves. The sinful nature wants to do evil, which is just the opposite of what the Spirit wants. And the Spirit gives us desires that are the opposite of what the sinful nature desires. These two

> *forces are constantly fighting each other, so you are not free to carry out your good intentions* (Gal. 5:16–17).

When we are "tuned in" to the Holy Spirit, we no longer hear many of the appeals of our sinful nature—not because they are no longer present but because they pale in comparison to the Holy Spirit's voice. However, we must continually fine-tune our sensitivity to the Holy Spirit through prayer and Bible reading.

When we walk according to God's commands rather than our lusts and passions, we release the Holy Spirit to lead us. Moreover, we experience an increasing desire to be led by Him. There are many ways we can adjust our minds to tune in to the voice of the Holy Spirit:

- We can read and memorize the Bible, which is the Word of God (Psa. 119:9–11). The Bible reveals God's heart and mind, and it teaches us how to please Him.
- We can surround ourselves with godly influences (Heb. 13:7). The apostle Paul encouraged the Philippian Christians to grow in their relationship with God by following the example of his own life (Php. 4:8–9). Likewise, the apostle Paul taught the Hebrew Christians to challenge and encourage each other toward love and good works (Heb. 10:24–25).
- We can submit ourselves to those who have spiritual authority over us, such as our pastors (Heb. 13:17).
- We can confess and repent of every sin God brings to mind (Acts 24:16; 1 Pet. 1:14–16; 1 John 1:9).
- We can draw close to God in obedient submission, and He will draw near to us (James 4:7–8).

- We can ask God for greater sensitivity toward, and reliance upon, the Holy Spirit (Luke 11:13; Eph. 5:18; 1 John 5:14–15).
- We can pray (Eph. 6:18). Every healthy relationship requires frequent and effective communication. When we pray, we are talking to God. This builds our relationship with Him, and it can align our hearts with His. As pastor, missionary, and author Henry Blackaby says, "We are filled with the Holy Spirit through prayer. When I get up from my knees, I am a different person than when I first went to prayer."[68]

If we hope to see cultural transformation, then we must rely upon the Holy Spirit's guidance. As such, becoming God's cultural influencers requires that we tune in to the Holy Spirit by intentionally seeking His voice and guidance in our lives.

CHAPTER 56

BEGINNING OUR INCREDIBLE JOURNEY

The apostle Paul encourages the Corinthian believers, *"You should imitate me, just as I imitate Christ"* (1 Cor. 11:1). What a bold claim! Yet when we study the life of Paul, we see that he truly did exemplify extraordinary Christlikeness. This is because Paul successfully internalized each of the principles we've examined for becoming God's cultural influencers.

So thoroughly had Paul internalized these principles that it seems everywhere he travelled either a revival or a riot occurred. Paul was highly informed and incredibly vocal. Never was there a doubt where he stood on any given matter—even if that position was likely to result in persecution and great suffering on his part. If ever there was a powerful example of a Christian faithfully contrasting the world, it is Paul. Likewise, if ever there was an example of how transformative the faithfulness of one man equipped with the truth of God's Word and the power of the Holy Spirit can be, it was Paul.

Nothing beyond ourselves is preventing us from having an impactful ministry like that of Paul. God can use each of us to transform our communities if we are willing, and if we are faithful. All that remains is for us to count the cost and determine whether we are willing to undertake this incredible journey, as Jesus teaches:

> *"If you do not carry your own cross and follow me, you cannot be my disciple.*
>
> *But don't begin until you count the cost. For who would begin construction of a building without first calculating the cost to see if there is enough money to finish it? Otherwise, you might complete only the foundation before running out of money, and then everyone would laugh at you. They would say, 'There's the person who started that building and couldn't afford to finish it!'*
>
> *Or what king would go to war against another king without first sitting down with his counselors to discuss whether his army of 10,000 could defeat the 20,000 soldiers marching against him? And if he can't, he will send a delegation to discuss terms of peace while the enemy is still far away. So you cannot become my disciple without giving up everything you own"* (Luke 14:27–33).

Having counted the cost, are we ready to begin our heavenly assignment of serving as God's cultural influencers? Are we adventurous enough to step out in faith and begin a journey to cultural transformation? The Chinese philosopher Lao Tzu once said, "A journey of a thousand miles begins with a single step."[69] Over the course of many chapters, we've examined several steps. Let us then begin this incredible journey by choosing to take our first step.

Part 6

BECOMING PREPARED

CHAPTER 57

PREPARED, NOT PREPPERS

Each of us live and minister in the shadow of divine judgment. We understand that God's corrective judgment permits seasons of national difficulty for the purpose of alerting us to the consequences of our continued rebellion and to provoke us to repentance. Knowing this, we should anticipate times of increasing difficulty in America. Apart from systemic cultural change, divinely permitted seasons of national trouble are likely inevitable, but this does not absolve us from our responsibility to minster during such seasons. Instead, it could be during these times of difficulty that our ministry is most effective—if we are prepared.

America has no shortage of people who are prepared for times of extreme difficulty. Often referred to as "preppers," these are survivalists who are determined to persevere through even the most dire circumstances. Such preppers typically focus on a particular facet of the feared apocalypse:

- **Doomsday** preppers have bunkers and fallout shelters designed to survive a nuclear holocaust.

- **Zombie apocalypse** preppers have enough guns, ammunition, and explosives to fend-off any invading force.
- **Biological warfare** preppers have masks, hazmat suits, medical supplies, and hermetically sealed shelters.
- **EMP** (electro-magnetic pulse) preppers have faraday cages and hand-powered tools.
- **Global warming** preppers have houses built high above sea level and far from the rising coastlines.
- **Financial collapse** preppers have stashes of gold, silver, and cryptocurrencies.

A defining mentality among such preppers is a will to survive at all costs. The world around them may disintegrate and perish, but they are survivors. However, this is not the mentality or kind of preparation necessary to *minister* through times of national difficulty.

As Christians, our goal should not be to simply survive. We have been commissioned to expand God's kingdom by teaching others to give their allegiance to God. Jesus commanded His followers, *"Go and make disciples of all the nations, baptizing them in the name of the Father and the Son and the Holy Spirit. Teach these new disciples to obey all the commands I have given you"* (Matt. 28:19–20b). Our goal ought to be to minister to others—regardless of our circumstances.

As Christians, our future is far more glorious than anything this present life has to offer (Rom. 8:18; 1 Cor. 2:9; 1 Pet. 1:3–5). By relentlessly clinging to life, we only delay this future; therefore, there must be something that merits preserving this life in trying times. The apostle Paul expresses this mentality in his letter to the Philippians:

> *I trust that my life will bring honor to Christ, whether I live or die. For to me, living means living for Christ, and dying is even better. But if I live, I can do more fruitful work for Christ. So I really don't know which is better. I'm torn between the two desires: I long to go and be with Christ, which would be far better for me. But for your sakes, it is better that I continue to live.*
>
> *Knowing this, I am convinced that I will remain alive so I can continue to help all of you grow and experience the joy of your faith* (Php. 1:20b–25).

Paul would have rejected the apocalyptic prepper mentality of surviving at all costs. Freed from his responsibility to minister to others, Paul would have had no reason to cling to this life. Likewise, our focus ought to be on ministry rather than survival. Therefore, when we speak of the need to prepare for times of increasing difficulty, we are endorsing a far different mentality and objective than that of the stereotypical American "prepper."

CHAPTER 58

PREPARING OTHERS WITH HOPE

As heralds of God's judgment, forerunners risk being labelled "doom-and-gloomers." From a biblical perspective, this title is fitting. The prophet Amos warns that the day of God's judgment will be a day of doom and gloom for the wicked: *"It is darkness, and not light, as if a man fled from a lion, and a bear met him, or went into the house and leaned his hand against the wall, and a serpent bit him. Is not the day of the LORD darkness, and not light, and gloom with no brightness in it?"* (Amos 5:18b–20, ESV). However, the phrase "doom-and-gloom" carries a far more nuanced meaning in our modern society that stands in stark contrast to the message of a forerunner.

In our modern context, doom-and-gloomers are overly pessimistic fearmongers who preach disaster without hope. Like Chicken Little, who is famous for being so anxious that a single drop of rain convinced her that sky was falling, anxious doom-and-gloomers default to a worst-case scenario with every hint of a burgeoning season of national difficulty. A rumor of war, a dip in the stock market, a rise in the cost of living, the threat of a pandemic, a lost election, a Supreme Court ruling, or any number of other setbacks become evidence that the end of life as we know it lurks just around the corner. Always emphasizing the negative, they offer no solutions and no hope. At best, they suggest the possibility of an animalistic survival among the strongest and most prepared. In contrast, the message of a forerunner is fundamentally hopeful—even when warning about the devastating consequences of rejecting God's moral instructions.

In even His most severe judgments, God used His people to emphasize the hope that accompanies repentance. Before declaring the gloom and doom accompanying divine judgment, Amos preached, *"Do what is good and run from evil so that you may live! Then the LORD God of Heaven's Armies will be your helper, just as you have claimed. Hate evil and love what is good; turn your courts into true halls of justice. Perhaps even yet the LORD God of Heaven's Armies will have mercy on the remnant of his people"* (Amos 5:14–15). Similarly, when proclaiming the day of the Lord, the apostle Peter explains, *"The Lord isn't really being slow about his promise [of judgment], as some people think. No, he is being patient for your sake. He does not want anyone to be destroyed, but wants everyone to repent."* (2 Pet. 3:9).

God's heart is not to see His creation destroyed. God's heart is to see people live righteous and abundant lives. Therefore, He does not need heralds proclaiming America's inevitable doom. Instead, He needs ministers whose warning message is intended to call people to repentance. As such, our warning message ought also to be hopeful.

Regardless of our circumstances, we join Amos in exhorting others to *"seek good, and not evil"* (Amos 5:14). Moreover, we boldly proclaim, "*The name of the LORD is a strong fortress; the godly run to him and are safe*" (Prov. 18:10). However, this promise is both hopeful and a dire warning to those who refuse to repent because, *"The way of the LORD is a stronghold to those with integrity, but it destroys the wicked"* (Prov. 10:29, emphasis added).

As forerunners of God's judgment, we warn people with the hope that they will repent; therefore, we cannot adopt the mentality of doom-and-gloomers. No matter how dire our national future appears, we must never forget that we are the ones tasked with proclaiming God's *good* news and offering the *hope* of a glorious future. Fundamentally, our warning is a call to respond in faith. Our job is not to emphasize how bad things will get but to warn that only the righteous will be safe from God's judgment.

CHAPTER 59

WINTER IS COMING

Winter is coming. Long before author George R.R. Martin popularized this phrase, it was a biblical warning:

Take a lesson from the ants, you lazybones.
Learn from their ways and become wise!
Though they have no prince
or governor or ruler to make them work,
they labor hard all summer,
gathering food for the winter.
But you, lazybones, how long will you sleep?
When will you wake up?
A little extra sleep, a little more slumber,
a little folding of the hands to rest—
then poverty will pounce on you like a bandit;
scarcity will attack you like an armed robber (Prov. 6:6–11).

There are seasons of plenty, and there are seasons of want. Sometimes they are unanticipated, but often they can be foreseen, and it is wise to plan ahead and take actions to prepare based upon what we know about these seasons.

Lean times are a reality of life. King Solomon's proverb addresses the concerns of an agrarian society, but in our modern American context, we might consider other hazardous seasons that can be reasonably anticipated. Economically, we anticipate seasons of inflation and deflation, seasons of collapsing markets, and bear market seasons. Some areas of the country anticipate seasons of increased natural disasters, such as hurricanes, wildfires, and tornadoes. Other areas of the country anticipate health concerns like an allergy season, or a cold and flu season. Awaiting and preparing for hazardous seasons of life is both natural and prudent.

Elsewhere, Solomon warns, *"A prudent person foresees danger and takes precautions. The simpleton goes blindly on and suffers the consequences"* (Prov. 22:3). The Bible encourages us to prepare for lean and difficult times, and it speaks poorly of those who either blind themselves to reality or who simply refuse to do anything about it. Perhaps we do not need to prepare to weather the apocalypse, but we ought to be prepared to withstand seasons of disruption to our nation's supply chain, an unforeseen injury, an inability to find work, a period of inflation, a natural disaster, or any number of other difficulties. Winter is coming, and we have a responsibility to be prepared when it arrives.

CHAPTER 60

STOCKPILING TREASURE IN HEAVEN

Some of the Bible's most beloved characters were prepared for disaster; however, their preparation was not rooted in a need to survive at all costs. Instead, their preparation was done from a sense of faithfulness to God and ministry to others:

- **Noah** prepared a shelter. He built an ark in preparation for a global flood that God was sending as judgment (Gen. 6).
- **Joseph** stored food. He prepared for famine during Egypt's years of plentiful harvests, thus ensuring that Egypt had enough grain to feed not only itself but its neighbors (Gen. 41).
- **Moses** essentially told the Israelites to prepare bug-out bags. They were to eat the Passover meal

prepared to travel at a moment's notice because their salvation was at hand (Exo. 12:11).

Despite a similarity in methods, these men stand apart from today's preppers because their reliance was not on their instincts and the thoroughness of their preparation but on God's faithfulness. They did not prepare because they had an inexplicable sense of doom. Instead, they prepared as an act of faith in response to God's revelation.

While it is prudent to be prepared to weather temporary seasons of disruption and difficulty, preparing for the apocalypse is another matter. Even if a time of severe judgment lays ahead for our nation, in the absence of God's clear revelation concerning America's future, doomsday preparation may contravene our faith in God's provision and encourage us to mistakenly place our confidence in the assets we have stored. Jesus cautions, "'*Don't store up treasures here on earth, where moths eat them and rust destroys them, and where thieves break in and steal. Store you treasures in heaven, where moths and rust cannot destroy, and thieves do not break in and steal. Wherever your treasure is, there the desires of your heart will also be*'" (Matt. 6:19–21).

Contrary to the mindset of many of today's preppers, Jesus says, *I tell you not to worry about everyday life—whether you have enough food to eat or enough clothes to wear. For life is more than food, and your body more than clothing*" (Luke 12:22b). Furthermore, He encourages His followers, "'*Sell your possessions and give to those in need. This will store up treasure for you in heaven!*'" because,

"Wherever your treasure is, there the desires of your heart will also be" (Luke 12:33a, 34).

Preparation is biblical (Prov. 22:3), but doomsday preparation, apart from God's special revelation, is not. It is rooted in a mindset of fear that is not from God (2 Tim. 1:7) and that undermines Jesus' instructions. Therefore, the only doomsday prepping we should be doing is preparing to stand before our holy God (Matt. 7:21–23; Rev. 20:11–15). We simply cannot allow a sense of dread to excuse anchoring our hearts to tangible assets that perish. Instead, let us use our resources and energy to store up treasures in heaven while stocking away just enough on earth to safeguard ourselves, and possibly others, against temporary difficulties.

CHAPTER 61

STANDING FIRM

Although self-defense, food storage, and healthcare are biblical principles, God has not instructed His people to prepare for the future with guns, food, and medicine. Instead, Jesus instructs us to stand firm in our faith amid a hostile culture of wickedness and to prepare for spiritual deception:

> *Don't let anyone mislead you, for many will come in my name, claiming, "I am the Messiah." They will deceive many. ... Then you will be arrested, persecuted, and killed. You will be hated all over the world because you are my followers. And many will turn away from me and betray and hate each other. And many false prophets will appear and will deceive many people. Sin will be rampant and everywhere, and the love of many will grow cold. But the one who endures to the end will be saved* (Matt. 24:4–5, 9–13).

Anyone who spends more time preparing for the future with guns, food, and medicine than preparing their faith for times of adversity is disregarding God's revelation. If we wish to be faithful to Jesus, then our primary concern ought to be preparing our minds and souls to discern spiritual truth and to stand firm amid a hostile culture of wickedness. Only after we have begun to address this primary threat should we focus on secondary threats, such as emergency food, shelter, and safety.

Being adequately prepared to stand firm through times of difficulty involves more than ensuring that we can fill our stomachs. We need to prepare to feed our souls as well. Are we as intentional about collecting good Bible study resources as we are about storing food? Are we as intentional about familiarizing ourselves with God's Word as we are about familiarizing ourselves with our weapons? Are we as intentional about applying God's truth to life issues as we are about learning medical applications?

Like Timothy, we should take the necessary steps to *"be prepared, whether the time is favorable or not"* to *"preach the word of God,"* and to *"patiently correct, rebuke, and encourage"* others with God's truth (2 Tim. 4:2). Similarly, let us aspire to so internalize the apostle Paul's final advice to the Thessalonians that it becomes second nature to us, whether we are experiencing times of peace or times of difficulty:

> *Honor those who are your leaders in the Lord's work. ... Show them great respect and wholehearted love because of their work. And live peacefully with each other.*

Brothers and sisters, we urge you to warn those who are lazy. Encourage those who are timid. Take tender care of those who are weak. Be patient with everyone.

See that no one pays back evil for evil, but always try to do good to each other and to all people.

Always be joyful. Never stop praying. Be thankful in all circumstances, for this is God's will for you who belong to Christ Jesus.

Do not stifle the Holy Spirit. Do not scoff at prophecies, but test everything that is said. Hold on to what is good. Stay away from every kind of evil (1 Thess. 5:12a, 13–22).

If we struggle with any part of this list in times of peace and stability, then we have little reason to believe that we will stand firm in that area during times of difficulty. However we choose to prepare for the future, let us prioritize internalizing this list so that we can stand firm, regardless of our circumstances.

CHAPTER 62

PREPARING TO MINISTER

Our great commission is not paused during times of trouble. Regardless of our circumstances, we are called to faithfully represent God, to make new disciples, and to teach them to obey God (Matt. 28:18–20; 2 Cor. 5:20). In other words, we are never absolved from our responsibility to bring people's thinking on moral matters into conformity with God's instructions. Therefore, any meaningful preparation plan must include a strategy for ministering through times of great difficulty.

Airline passengers are told, in the event of an emergency, to place the oxygen mask on themselves before helping others. This is because we cannot help others if we are incapacitated. Similarly, if our faith is unable to persevere through times of trial, we will be incapacitated as God's representatives. Therefore, we must prepare now to stand firm in the face of adversity. This not only involves preparing ourselves physically but also mentally, emotionally, morally, and spiritually.

The apostle Paul encourages us:

Be strong in the Lord and in his mighty power. Put on all of God's armor so that you will be able to stand firm against all strategies of the devil. For we are not fighting against flesh-and-blood enemies, but against evil rulers and authorities of the unseen world, against mighty powers in this dark world, and against evil spirits in the heavenly places.

Therefore, put on every piece of God's armor so you will be able to resist the enemy in the time of evil. Then after the battle you will still be standing firm. Stand your ground, putting on the belt of truth and the body armor of God's righteousness. For shoes, put on the peace that comes from the Good News so that you will be fully prepared. In addition, to all of these, hold up the shield of faith to stop the fiery arrows of the devil. Put on salvation as your helmet, and take the sword of the Spirit, which is the word of God.

Pray in the Spirit at all times and on every occasion. Stay alert and be persistent in your prayers for all believers everywhere (Eph. 6:10b–18).

We ought to use times of relative stability to prepare ourselves to resist the temptations that are exacerbated in times of difficulty: compromise, selfishness, ruthlessness, depression, dishonesty, lawlessness, violence, etc. If we struggle with these temptations in good times, what reason do we have to believe that we will remain faithful in bad times? Likewise, if we are unsure of God's promises in stable times, what makes us believe we will remain faithful in times of adversity? We should use the present to gain answers to any spiritual questions and doubts that might undermine our faith in times of difficulty.

Our goal in all of this is not merely to stand firm for our own sake. Rather, our goal is to stand firm in the face of adversity so that we can effectively minister to others in all circumstances.

CHAPTER 63

GOD'S PREPARATION PLAN

As Americans, we are particularly inclined toward self-reliance. Personal ownership and independence rest at the heart of the American dream, but God does not call His people to be self-reliant. We certainly have a responsibility to seek to provide for our own needs (1 Thess. 3:6–12), but in the earliest days of the church, the people also *"felt that what they owned was not their own, so they shared everything they had. ... There were no needy people among them, because those who owned land or houses would sell them and bring the money to the apostles to give to those in need"* (Acts 4:32b, 34).

This is God's preparation plan for His people: Christians caring for the needs of one another. Among His people, God often uses the surplus of some to meet the needs of others. When raising money for the needs of those in the church at Jerusalem, the apostle Paul explained:

Give according to what you have, not what you don't have. Of course, I don't mean your giving should make life easy for others and hard for yourselves. I only mean that there should be some equality. Right now you have plenty and can help those who are in need. Later, they will have plenty and can share with you when you need it. In this way, things will be equal. As the Scriptures say,

"Those who gathered a lot had nothing left over,
and those who gathered only a little had enough"

(2 Cor. 8:12b–15).

Investing in the needs of others is a kind of heavenly insurance policy. It is our best means of preparing for whatever may await us in the future. However, our generosity ought not to be limited to Christians. Contrary to a popular narrative that, during a time of national crisis, Christians should be prepared to kill and to heartlessly deny provisions to people in their time of greatest need, we should be prepared to share with everyone—even those who foolishly refused to prepare for times of difficulty. After all, what better opportunity will we be given to minister to others? If we are prepared to meet people's physical needs, then we will likely gain the opportunity to provide for their spiritual needs as well.

Of course, such generosity risks producing times of great personal discomfort. Nonetheless, may we be like the church in Macedonia who was so eager to provide for the church in Jerusalem that the people gave beyond their means. The apostle Paul explains:

They are being tested by many troubles, and they are very poor. But they are also filled with abundant joy, which has overflowed in rich generosity.

For I can testify that they gave not only what they could afford, but far more. And they did it of their own free will. They begged us again and again for the privilege of sharing in the gift for the believers in Jerusalem. They even did more than we had hoped, for their first action was to give themselves to the Lord and to us, just as God wanted them to do" (2 Cor. 8:2–5).

It may cost us our comfort and security, but we should be prepared to share our abundance with anyone in need. Moreover, we should resist the temptation to go "off the grid" and to isolate ourselves because we may be an important part of God's plan to provide for others and because we should always want to remain in a position where we can minister to others and fulfill our great commission (Matt. 28:18–20). Ministry ought to be our priority, not material possessions or self-preservation.

As stewards of God's resources, our responsibility is to dispense God's blessings in a manner that is consistent with His heart. If He pleases, God may always choose to grant us more provisions. Certainly, the God who preserved the Israelite's clothes and sandals in the wilderness can preserve our equipment, if He pleases (Deut. 29:5). The God who used two loaves of bread and five fish to feed 5,000 men can multiply our supplies, if He pleases (Matt. 14:16–21). And the God who supplied the widow's jar of flour can stretch our provisions, if He pleases (1 Kings 17:8–16).

When we are generous to those in need, we accurately represent God's heart, and we participate in *His* preparation plan. It may not conform to conventional wisdom, but God's preparation plan is based in selfless generosity, not self-centered hoarding. Paul concludes:

> *Remember this—a farmer who plants only a few seeds will get a small crop. But the one who plants generously will get a generous crop. You must each decide in your heart how much to give. And don't give reluctantly or in response to pressure. "For God loves a person who gives cheerfully." And God will generously provide all you need. Then you will always have everything you need and plenty left over to share with others. As the Scriptures say,*
>
> *"They share freely and give generously to the poor.*
> *Their good deeds will be remembered forever"* (2 Cor. 9:6–9).

CHAPTER 64

THE GOD FACTOR

Following Jesus often contravenes conventional wisdom. Far from instructing us to prepare for every contingency, Jesus calls His followers to trust Him enough to go wherever He leads: *"As they were walking along, someone said to Jesus, 'I will follow you wherever you go.' But Jesus replied, 'Foxes have dens to live in, and birds have nests, but the Son of Man has no place even to lay his head'"* (Luke 9:57–58). Often, our future is uncertain, and we may have no idea from where our provisions will come. Indeed, in some instances, Jesus may even ask us to relinquish everything we own: *"Looking at the man, Jesus felt genuine love for him. 'There is still one thing you haven't done,' he told him. 'Go and sell all your possessions and give the money to the poor, and you will have treasure in heaven. Then come, follow me'"* (Mark 10:21).

Terrifying as such a prospect may be, it can also be liberating. Sometimes our possessions can anchor us or make us reluctant to obey the voice of God. Consider for a moment: Should we prepare an ideal homestead capable of sustaining life off the grid, would we be willing to up-and-move if God asked? Sometimes our preparation can limit how we are willing to serve God and can interfere with our ability to lean wholly upon Him.

When challenged, where does our hope truly rest? Have we made our preparations accordingly? In our minds, have we afforded the possibility that God may defy conventional wisdom in His provision for us?

As Christians, we should never underestimate the God factor. It always remains God's prerogative to supernaturally:

- **Provide**, like He did for the widow in debt (2 Kings 4:1–7)
- **Protect**, like He did for the Israelites as they fought the Amalekites (Exo. 17:8–13)
- **Heal**, like He did for the high priest's servant (Luke 22:50–51)
- **Shelter**, like He did for those dwelling in the land of Goshen (Exo. 8:22; 9:26)
- **Embolden**, like He did for Peter and John when testifying before the ruling council (Acts 4:8–13)
- **Enlighten**, like Jesus promised His followers (John 14:26; Luke 12:11–12)

We have no reason to fear the future if we are faithfully pursuing God. For some of us, this may involve thorough preparation, while others may be called to follow a different path of obedience. Indeed, it may be that our particular season of life, and the ministry to which some of us are called, does not afford opportunity to adequately prepare for lean and difficult periods. Nonetheless, we can be confident that the most secure place to be is in faithful obedience to whatever God has called us to do. Despite our circumstances, we can be faithful because we know that God is faithful toward us (2 Thess. 3:3; 2 Tim. 2:13). Therefore, let us have the confidence of the apostle Paul who assured the Christians in Philippi, *"And this same God who takes care of me will supply all your needs from his glorious riches, which have been given to us in Christ Jesus"* (Php. 4:19).

CONCLUSION

CONCLUSION

COMPELLED TO WARN

As representatives of God, every one of us is called to be a forerunner who is willing to publicly share God's heart for America. Moreover, the message of a forerunner is inextricably linked with our commission from Jesus to make disciples of all nations and to teach them to obey His instructions (Matt. 28:19–20). However, "forerunner" is not a synonym for "Christian." Not every Christian identifies as a forerunner. What distinguishes a forerunner from other gospel-minded Christians is an awareness of the role that nations play in God's redemptive plan to draw the hearts of people to Himself and a burden to warn others about God's judgment upon rebellious nations that push people away from God. A forerunner emphasizes the importance of not only individual righteousness, but also of *collective* righteousness.

Simply put, a forerunner is a cultural influencer who delivers God's warning of national judgment with the goal of eliciting a spirit of repentance that will ripple into cultural change among both individuals and their communities. At the heart of this appeal is the transformative power of the gospel. A forerunner hopes for the blessings associated with repentance, but like the prophet Amos, a forerunner also fearlessly warns the rebellious, *"Prepare to meet your God in judgment"* (Amos 4:12b).

We do not know when this moment may come—only that our holy and just God will not ignore rebellion to His moral instructions indefinitely. For individuals, the forerunner message is a call to honestly evaluate our relationship with God and to repent of any attitudes and habits that interfere with our faithfulness to Him. For communities, the forerunner message is a call to make systemic cultural changes that embrace God's moral standard.

God has equipped each of us with talents and spiritual gifts, varied passions and interests, and unique experiences. These will inevitably influence the way we choose to lean into the task of warning others and calling them to respond in faith. Some may choose to emphasize the warning stronger than others. There simply is no one-size-fits-all approach to warning. Just as God uses a wide variety of approaches among churches and individuals to share His gospel with a broad array of personalities, so also God uses forerunners of all stripes to communicate His warning message to Americans of all persuasions. Today, God is calling His diverse forerunners to run ahead, in America, to prepare each of these personality types to meet their God.

A gospel presentation without the cross and individual righteousness is not the gospel, and a forerunner message without a warning of national judgment and collective righteousness is not a forerunner message. As we preach the gospel, contrast the culture, and endeavor to influence the way people think about moral matters, we cannot lose sight of the fact that, fundamentally, a forerunner warns. Let us then rise to the challenge—not with a spirit of fear, judgmentalism, or cynicism, but with a spirit that balances our grief over national waywardness with a hope that individuals and nations will, indeed, prepare themselves to meet our holy and just God before He arrives in judgment.

END NOTES

1. Abraham Lincoln, "Second Inaugural Address," Speech, *Abraham Lincoln Online*, [March 4, 1865], Accessed July 29, 2022, https://www.abrahamlincolnonline.org/lincoln/speeches/inaug2.htm.

2. Abraham Lincoln, "Proclamation Appointing a National Fast Day," Speech, *Abraham Lincoln Online*, [March 30, 1863], Accessed July 29, 2022. https://www.abrahamlincolnonline.org/lincoln/speeches/fast.htm.

3. Henry Morris, *God and the Nations* (Green Forest: Master Books, 2005), 29.

4. Morris, 29–30.

5. Andy Patton, "Why Did God Flood the World?" *Bible Project*, 2020, https://bibleproject.com/blog/why-did-god-flood-the-world/.

6. Henry Morris, *God and the Nations* (Green Forest: Master Books, 2005), 35.

7. John Thompson, *New American Commentary*, "The Reformation (15:8–15)," Logos Bible Software, Accessed January 27, 2022.

8. "American Worldview Inventory 2020 – At a Glance," 1, Arizona Christian University: Cultural Research Center, March 24, 2020,

https://www.arizonachristian.edu/wp-content/uploads/2020/03/CRC_AWVI2020_Report.pdf.

9. "Probe's Religious Views and Practices 2020: Do Christians Believe in Christ as the Only Savior of the World?" n.d., Accessed January 5, 2022, https://files.constantcontact.com/dbebe121701/f4881dec-45ca-4cdb-a997-5b3709f9ed02.pdf.

10. "American Worldview Inventory 2020 – At a Glance," 3, Arizona Christian University: Cultural Research Center, March 24, 2020, https://www.arizonachristian.edu/wp-content/uploads/2020/03/CRC_AWVI2020_Report.pdf.

11. "American Worldview Inventory 2020 – At a Glance," 2.

12. Jeff Diamant, "Half of U.S. Christians Say Casual Sex between Consenting Adults Is Sometimes or Always Acceptable," *Pew Research Center*, August 31, 2020, https://www.pewresearch.org/fact-tank/2020/08/31/half-of-u-s-christians-say-casual-sex-between-consenting-adults-is-sometimes-or-always-acceptable/.

13. Heather Clark, "Survey Finds Half of Professing Christians Think Sex outside of Marriage Is Sometimes or Always Okay," *Christian News*, September 5, 2020, https://christiannews.net/2020/09/05/survey-finds-half-of-professing-christians-think-sex-outside-of-marriage-is-sometimes-or-always-okay/.

14. "Pastors' Views on Moral Failure: Survey of American Protestant Pastors," *Lifeway Research*, 2019, http://lifewayresearch.com/wp-content/uploads/2020/08/Pastors-Moral-Failure.pdf.

15. Leah MarieAnn Klett, "Most Pastors Say Adultery Shouldn't Permanently Disqualify Clergy from Ministry: Survey," *Christian Post*, August 12, 2020, https://www.christianpost.com/news/most-pastors-say-

committing-adultery-shouldnt-permanently-disqualify-clergy-from-ministry-survey.html.

16. "Public Opinion on Abortion," *Pew Research Center*, May 6, 2021, https://www.pewforum.org/fact-sheet/public-opinion-on-abortion/.

17. "State of Theology," *Ligonier Ministries*, 2020, https://thestateoftheology.com.

18. "Probe's Religious Views and Practices 2020: Do Christians Believe in Christ as the Only Savior of the World?" 5, *Barna Group*, n.d., Accessed January 5, 2022, https://files.constantcontact.com/dbebe121701/f4881dec-45ca-4cdb-a997-5b3709f9ed02.pdf.

19. Barack Obama, "'Call to Renewal' Keynote Address," *Obama Speeches*, June 28, 2006, http://www.obamaspeeches.com/081-Call-to-Renewal-Keynote-Address-Obama-Speech.htm.

20. Robxz, "Obama: We Are No Longer a Christian Nation," YouTube video, 0:17. March 9, 2008, https://www.youtube.com/watch?v=tmC3IevZiik.

21. Mitchell Landsberg, "Evangelical Leaders Echo Obama, Say U.S. Not a Christian Nation," Politics, *Los Angeles Times*, July 31, 2012, 12:00 a.m., PT, https://www.latimes.com/politics/la-xpm-2012-jul-31-la-pn-evangelical-leaders-echo-obama-say-us-not-a-christian-nation-20120731-story.html.

22. Jon Meacham, "Meacham: The End of Christian America," Culture, *Newsweek*, February 2, 2022, https://www.newsweek.com/meacham-end-christian-america-77125.

23. Jon Meacham, "A Nation of Christians Is Not a Christian Nation," Opinion, *New York Times*, October 7, 2007, https://www.nytimes.com/2007/10/07/opinion/07meacham.html.

24. Norman Wirzba, "Why We Can Now Declare the End of 'Christian America,'" Opinion, *Washington Post*, February 25, 2016, https://www.washingtonpost.com/news/acts-of-faith/wp/2016/02/25/why-we-can-now-declare-the-end-of-christian-america/.

25. Robert Jones, "White Christian America Ended in the 2010s," Opinion, *NBC News*, December 27, 2019, 12:06 p.m., EST, https://www.nbcnews.com/think/opinion/2010s-spelled-end-white-christian-america-ncna1106936.

26. Neda Semnani, "Americans Obsessed with Their Own Happiness Overlook the Key Ingredient to a Good Life," News, *Washington Post*, October 7, 2016, 7:00 a.m., EDT, https://www.washingtonpost.com/news/inspired-life/wp/2016/10/07/americans-obsessed-with-their-own-happiness-overlook-the-key-ingredient-to-a-good-life.

27. Christopher Ingraham, "Americans Are Becoming Less Happy, and There's Research to Prove It," Science, *Los Angeles Times*, March 23, 2019, 5:00 a.m., PT, https://www.latimes.com/science/sciencenow/la-sci-sn-americans-less-happy-20190323-story.html.

28. Alexa Tsoulis-Reay, "What It's Like to Date a Horse," *New York Magazine*, November 20, 2014, Accessed November 21, 2014, http://nymag.com/scienceofus/2014/11/what-its-like-to-date-a-horse.html.

29. Matthew Impelli, "Condoms Placed in Elementary Schools Sparks Online Debate," US, *Newsweek*, July 6, 2021, 6:00 p.m., EDT, https://www.newsweek.com/condoms-placed-elementary-schools-sparks-online-debate-1607352.

30. "Vaccine (Shot) for Human Papillomavirus," *Centers for Disease Control and Prevention*, n.d., Accessed January 5, 2022, https://www.cdc.gov/vaccines/parents/diseases/hpv.html.

31. Ashley McGuire, "Most Americans Don't Want a Standing Ovation for Abortions Until Birth. But Democrats Do," Opinion, *USA*

Today, January 30, 2019, 6:00 a.m., ET, https://www.usatoday.com/story/opinion/2019/01/30/new-york-abortion-law-liberal-leaders-celebration-death-life-column/2670049002/.

32. Mike DeBonis and Felicia Sonmez, "Senate Blocks Bill on Medical Care for Children Born Alive after Attempted Abortion," Politics, *Washington Post*, February 25, 2019, https://www.washingtonpost.com/politics/senate-blocks-bill-on-medical-care-for-children-born-alive-after-attempted-abortion/2019/02/25/e5d3d4d8-3924-11e9-a06c-3ec8ed509d15_story.html.

33. Drag Queen Story Hour, https://www.dragqueenstoryhour.org.

34. "Libraries Respond: Drag Queen Story Hour," *American Library Association*, n.d., Accessed July 15, 2022, https://www.ala.org/advocacy/libraries-respond-drag-queen-story-hour.

35. Marina Villeneuve, "Maine Becomes 8th State to Legalize Assisted Suicide," *AP News*, June 12, 2019, https://apnews.com/article/legislation-augusta-health-us-news-ap-top-news-7f0fe9d789294a02852c1669c892f382.

36. "Needle Exchange Programs Promote Public Safety," *American Civil Liberties Union*, n.d., Accessed January 5, 2022, https://www.aclu.org/fact-sheet/needle-exchange-programs-promote-public-safety.

37. German Lopez, "Why Some US Cities Are Opening Safe Spaces for Injecting Heroin," Drugs, *CNBC News*, January 25, 2018, 12:06 p.m., EST, Last updated January 25, 2018, 12:06 p.m., EST, https://www.cnbc.com/2018/01/25/why-some-us-cities-are-opening-safe-spaces-for-injecting-heroin.html.

38. John MacArthur, "When God Abandons a Nation," Sermon, *Grace to Your*, August 20, 2006, https://www.gty.org/library/sermons-library/80-314/when-god-abandons-a-nation.

39. John Adams, "From John Adams to Massachusetts Militia, 11 October 1798," Letter, *National Archives: Founders Online*, n.d., Accessed January 6, 2022, https://founders.archives.gov/documents/Adams/99-02-02-3102.

40. Martin Luther King Jr., "A Knock at Midnight," Sermon, Mount Zion Baptist Church, 1967, Source: Eric Patterson, "Martin Luther King, Jr. on Power and Love," Religious Freedom Institute, January 15, 2021, https://www.religiousfreedominstitute.org/blog/martin-luther-king-jr-on-power-and-love.

41. "Faith in America Survey," 6, Marist Poll, *Deseret News*, March 22, 2022, https://thefederalist.com/wp-content/uploads/2022/03/watermark_Sections-1-3_Deseret-News-Faith-in-America-Survey-Summary-Report.pdf.

42. "Faith in America Survey," 7.

43. "Faith in America Survey," 9.

44. "Americans Have Positive Views about Religion's Role in Society, but Want It out of Politics," *Pew Research Center*, November 15, 2019, https://www.pewresearch.org/religion/2019/11/15/americans-have-positive-views-about-religions-role-in-society-but-want-it-out-of-politics.

45. Martin Luther King Jr., "A Knock at Midnight," Sermon, Mount Zion Baptist Church, 1967.

46. Alexandra DeSanctis, "How Democrats Purged 'Safe, Legal, Rare,' from the Party," Outlook, *Washington Post*, November 15, 2019, 4:19 p.m., EST, https://www.washingtonpost.com/outlook/how-democrats-purged-safe-legal-rare-from-the-party/2019/11/15/369af73c-01a4-11ea-8bab-0fc209e065a8_story.html.

47. Steven Ertelt, "19 States Allow Infanticide, Let Abortionists Leave Babies to Die Who Survive an Abortion," *Life News*, February

14, 2019, Accessed February 26, 2019, https://www.lifenews.com/2019/02/14/19-states-allow-infanticide-let-abortionists-leave-babies-to-die-who-survive-an-abortion.

48. Virginia Kruta, "Democrats Celebrate as Bill Compelling Doctors to Save Newborns Dies in the Senate," *Daily Caller,* February 26, 2019, Accessed February 27, 2019, https://dailycaller.com/2019/02/26/democrats-celebrate-born-alive-bill-dies-senate.

49. Olivia Summers, "Maryland Legislature Considers Sick Bill That Could Legalize Infanticide up to 28 Days AFTER Birth," Blog, *American Center for Law and Justice,* March 4, 2022, https://aclj.org/pro-life/maryland-legislature-considers-sick-bill-that-could-legalize-infanticide-up-to-28-days-after-birth.

50. Olivia Summers, "California Follows Maryland's Lead with Disturbing Bill That Could Effectively Legalize Infanticide," *American Center for Law and Justice,* March 28, 2022, https://aclj.org/pro-life/california-follows-marylands-lead-with-disturbing-bill-that-could-effectively-legalize-infanticide.

51. Eric Davis, "Should Christians Not Be Known for What They Are Against?" *Cripplegate,* March 20, 2019, https://thecripplegate.com/should-christians-not-be-known-for-what-they-are-against.

52. John MacArthur, "When God Abandons a Nation," Sermon, *Grace to You,* August 20, 2006, https://www.gty.org/library/sermons-library/80-314/when-god-abandons-a-nation.

53. Erwin Lutzer, *Is God on America's Side? The Surprising Answer and How It Affects Our Future* (Chicago: Moody Publishers, 2008), 72.

54. "The 2020 Census of American Religion," *Public Religion Research Institute,* July 8, 2021, https://www.prri.org/research/2020-census-of-american-religion.

55. John Adams, "From John Adams to Massachusetts Militia, 11 October 1798," Letter, *National Archives: Founders Online*, n.d., Accessed January 6, 2022, https://founders.archives.gov/documents/Adams/99-02-02-3102.

56. Michael Brown, "Love Warns," *AskDrBrown*, August 28, 2015, https://askdrbrown.org/library/love-warns.

57. *The Complete Word Study Dictionary, New Testament,* s.v. "topos" G5117, Word Study Series, Edited by Spiros Zodhiates, Revised ed., Chattanooga, AMG Publishers, 1993.

58. *The Complete Word Study Dictionary, New Testament,* s.v. "rhomphaia" G4501, Word Study Series, Edited by Spiros Zodhiates, Revised ed., Chattanooga, AMG Publishers, 1993.

59. *The Complete Word Study Dictionary, New Testament,* s.v. "machaira" G3162.

60. *The Complete Word Study Dictionary, New Testament,* s.v. "rhema" G4487.

61. *The Complete Word Study Dictionary, New Testament,* s.v. "rhema" G4487.

62. Blaise Pascal, *Pensees,* Trans. A.J. Krailsheimer (New York: Penguin, 1966), 320.

63. John Mark Comer, *God Has a Name* (Grand Rapids: Zondervan, 2017), 66, 68.

64. John Mark Comer, *God Has a Name*, 68.

65. Monique, "The History of the 'Two Wolves/Two Dogs' Story," *Moniquilliloquies*, February 15, 2012, https://tithenai.tumblr.com/post/17655980732/the-history-of-the-two-wolvestwo-dogs-story.

66. Billy Graham, *The Holy Spirit: Activating God's Power in Your Life* (United Kingdom: Thomas Nelson, 2011), 92.

67. Billy Graham, *The Holy Spirit: Activating God's Power in Your Life*, 92.

68. Henry Blackaby, Seek Week Conference at Life Action Ministries, n.d.

69. "Lao Tzu," *BBC*, October 27, 2006, https://web.archive.org/web/20061027065217/http://www.bbc.co.uk:80/worldservice/learningenglish/movingwords/shortlist/laotzu.shtml.

ALSO AVAILABLE

from Timothy Zebell & Dave Warn

Insurgence: The Revolutionary Nature of the Kingdom of God

The Bible is not only a story about Jesus' journey to the cross. It is also a story about God's Kingdom and mankind's role in that Kingdom. Due to our rebellion, we forfeited our role in God's Kingdom, but God is not content to relinquish what He began. Instead, He has chosen to redeem His creation. It is for this reason that Jesus began an insurgence more than 2,000 years ago. Uncover these amazing truths in Timothy Zebell and Dave Warn's Bible study, *Insurgence: The Revolutionary Nature of the Kingdom of God.*

"Fresh and thought-provoking. Articulate and precise. Prepare to be chewing on challenging insights for quite some time."

~Craig Anderson ChFC, Owner, Family Focused Financial

ALSO AVAILABLE

from Timothy Zebell

Culture of Lies: Understanding Fake News and Its Spiritual Ramifications

Nearly half of all Americans have a negative view of the news media. Only 44% say they can think of a news source that reports the news objectively, and 66% say news outlets do not do a good job of separating fact from opinion. Now we have a president who regularly calls mainstream news outlets "fake news."

- How did we get here?
- What is fake news?
- Who is truly to blame?
- Is the label fair?
- What are the spiritual ramifications of fake news?

"There has been more new error propagated by the press in the last ten years than in an hundred years before 1798."

~2nd President of the U.S. John Adams

"Nothing can now be believed which is seen in a newspaper. Truth itself becomes suspicious by being put into that polluted vehicle."

~3rd President of the U.S. Thomas Jefferson

"The press has become so dishonest that if we don't talk about it, we are doing a tremendous disservice to the American people."

~45th President of the U.S. Donald Trump

ALSO AVAILABLE

from Timothy Zebell

Unmasking Halloween: The Truth behind America's Trickiest Holiday & How to Navigate It

This mysterious holiday is as complex as it is ancient. No longer is Halloween the frivolous children's holiday that is had become by the mid-20th century. Today it is a commercial juggernaut and an indispensable component of American culture. How did a rural harvest festival become one of America's top commercial holidays? Until we understand the ways that Halloween's character and purpose have transformed over time, we will not know how best to navigate this enigmatic holiday.

- What are the origins of our monster lore, haunted houses, and trick or treat?
- What does the Bible say about vampires, werewolves, zombies, witches, and ghosts?
- Is Halloween a religious holiday or a secular celebration?
- Should Christians celebrate Halloween?
- How can Christians chart an approach to Halloween that is free from guilt and uncertainty?

Find all of Timothy Zebell's books and Bible studies at

www.Amazon.com

Or download them and his articles for FREE at

www.ForerunnersOfAmerica.com

Made in the USA
Coppell, TX
01 September 2023

21088349R00134